GENESIS 12–33

The Father of Israel

John MacArthur

THOMAS NELSON
Since 1798

MacArthur Bible Studies

Genesis 12–33: The Father of Israel

© 2015 by John MacArthur

Published in Nashville, Tennessee, by Nelson Books, an imprint of Thomas Nelson. Nelson Books and Thomas Nelson are registered trademarks of HarperCollins Christian Publishing, Inc.

Originally published in association with the literary agency of Wolgemuth & Associates, Inc. Original layout, design, and writing assistance by Gregory C. Benoit Publishing, Old Mystic, CT.

"Unleashing God's Truth, One Verse at a Time" is a trademark of Grace to You. All rights reserved.

Thomas Nelson, Inc. titles may be purchased in bulk for educational, business, fundraising, or sales promotional use. For information, please e-mail SpecialMarkets@ThomasNelson.com.

Scripture quotations are taken from *The New King James Version*. © 1982 by Thomas Nelson, Inc. Used by permission. All rights reserved.

Some material from the Introduction, "Keys to the Text" and "Exploring the Meaning" sections taken from *The MacArthur Bible Commentary*, John MacArthur, Copyright © 2005 Thomas Nelson Publishers.

ISBN 978-0-718-03456-6

First Printing December 2015 / Printed in the United States of America

HB 02.08.2024

CONTENTS

INTRODUCTION

The men known as "the patriarchs" in the Bible (Abraham, Isaac, and Jacob) lived during the Old Testament time before Israel's captivity in Egypt. They were the "fathers" of the Jewish people because their descendants became the nation of Israel. These men and their wives were also great saints of the faith—the faith that finds its fulfillment in the person and work of Jesus Christ.

Each was a real human being, made of the same flesh as you and me and with similar strengths and weaknesses. God also called each to a unique walk of faith and to face unique circumstances and challenges along the way. This is the very thing that unites them: every one of these patriarchs lived a life characterized by faith in God.

In these twelve studies, we will examine the biblical events depicted in Genesis 12–33. We will look at Abraham's call to live in Canaan, Sarah's act of faith in God's promise for a son (even at the age of ninety), Jacob's wrestling match with God, and more. Through it all, we will also learn some precious truths about the character of God, and we will see His great faithfulness in keeping His promises. We will learn, in short, what it means to walk by faith.

TITLE

The English title "Genesis" comes from the Septuagint (the Greek translation of the Bible) meaning "origins." Genesis serves to introduce the Pentateuch (the first five books of the Old Testament) and the entire Bible. The influence of Genesis in Scripture is demonstrated by the fact that it is quoted more than 35 times in the New Testament, with hundreds of allusions appearing in both Testaments. The story line of salvation, which begins in Genesis 3, is not completed until Revelation 21–22, where the eternal kingdom of redeemed believers is gloriously pictured.

AUTHOR AND DATE

While (1) the author does not identify himself in Genesis, and (2) Genesis ends almost three centuries before Moses was born, both the Old Testament and the New Testament ascribe this composition to Moses (see, e.g., Exodus 17:14; Numbers 33:2; Ezra 6:18; Nehemiah 13:1; Matthew 8:4; Mark 12:26; Luke 16:29; John 5:46). Moses is the fitting author in light of his educational background (see Acts 7:22), and no compelling reasons have been forthcoming to challenge his authorship. Genesis was written after the Exodus (c. 1445 BC) but before Moses' death (c. 1405 BC).

BACKGROUND AND SETTING

The initial setting for Genesis is eternity past. God, by willful act and divine Word, spoke all creation into existence, furnished it, and breathed life into a lump of dirt that He fashioned in His image to become Adam. God made mankind the crowning point of His creation; i.e., His companions who would enjoy fellowship with Him and bring glory to His name.

The historical background for the early events in Genesis is clearly Mesopotamian. While it is difficult to pinpoint precisely the historical moment for which this book was written, Israel first heard Genesis sometime prior to crossing the Jordan River and entering the Promised Land (c. 1405 BC).

Genesis has three distinct sequential geographical settings: (1) Mesopotamia (chapters 1–11); (2) the Promised Land (chapters 12–36); and (3) Egypt (chapters 37–50). The time frames of these three segments are: (1) creation to c. 2090 BC; (2) 2090–1897 BC; and (3) 1897–1804 BC. Genesis covers more time than the remaining books of the Bible combined.

HISTORICAL AND THEOLOGICAL THEMES

In this book of beginnings, God revealed Himself and a worldview to Israel that contrasted, at times sharply, with the worldview of Israel's neighbors. The author made no attempt to defend the existence of God or to present a systematic discussion of His person and works. Rather, Israel's God distinguished Himself clearly from the alleged gods of her neighbors. Theological foundations are revealed, which include God the Father, God the Son, God the Holy Spirit, man, sin, redemption, covenant, promise, Satan and angels, kingdom, revelation, Israel, judgment, and blessing.

Genesis 1–11 (primeval history) reveals the origins of the universe (the beginnings of time and space) and many of the firsts in human experience, such as marriage, family, the Fall, sin, redemption, judgment, and nations. Genesis 12–50 (patriarchal history) explained to Israel how they came into existence as a family whose ancestry could be traced to Eber (hence the "Hebrews"; see Genesis 10:24–25) and even more remotely to Shem, the son of Noah (hence the "Semites"; see Genesis 10:21). God's people came to understand not only their ancestry and family history but also the origins of their institutions, customs, languages, and different cultures, especially basic human experiences such as sin and death.

Because they were preparing to enter Canaan and dispossess the Canaanite inhabitants of their homes and properties, God revealed their enemies' background. In addition, they needed to understand the actual basis of the war they were about to declare in light of the immorality of killing, consistent with the other four books that Moses was writing (Exodus, Leviticus, Numbers, and Deuteronomy). Ultimately, the Jewish nation would understand a selected portion of preceding world history and the inaugural background of Israel as a basis by which they would live in their new beginnings under Joshua's leadership in the land that had previously been promised to Abraham, their original patriarchal forefather.

Genesis 12:1–3 established a primary focus on God's promises to Abraham. This narrowed their view from the entire world of peoples in Genesis 1–11 to one small nation, Israel, through whom God would progressively accomplish His redemptive plan. This underscored Israel's mission to be "a light for the Gentiles" (Isaiah 42:6). God promised land, descendants (seed), and blessing.

This threefold promise became, in turn, the basis of the covenant with Abraham (see Genesis 15:1–20). The rest of Scripture bears out the fulfillment of these promises.

On a larger scale, Genesis 1–11 sets forth a singular message about the character and works of God. In the sequence of accounts which make up these chapters of Scripture, a pattern emerges that reveals God's abundant grace as He responded to the willful disobedience of mankind. Without exception, in each account God increased the manifestation of His grace. But also without exception, man responded in greater sinful rebellion. In biblical words, the more sin abounded the more did God's grace abound (see Romans 5:20).

One final theme of both theological and historical significance that sets Genesis apart from other books of Scripture is that this first book of Scripture corresponds closely with the final book. In the book of Revelation, the paradise that was lost in Genesis will be regained. The apostle John clearly presented the events recorded in his book as future resolutions to the problems that began as a result of the curse in Genesis 3. His focus is on the effects of the Fall in the undoing of creation and the manner in which God rids His creation of the curse effect. In John's own words, "No longer will there be any curse" (Revelation 22:3). Not surprisingly, in the final chapter of God's Word, believers will find themselves back in the garden of Eden, the eternal paradise of God, eating from the tree of life (see Revelation 22:1–14). At that time they will partake, wearing robes washed in the blood of the Lamb (see 22:14).

INTERPRETIVE CHALLENGES

Grasping the individual messages of Genesis that make up the larger plan and purpose of the book presents no small challenge, because both the individual accounts and the book's overall message offer important lessons to faith and works. Genesis presents creation by divine fiat, *ex nihilo*; i.e., "out of nothing." Three traumatic events of epic proportions—namely the Fall, the universal flood, and the dispersion of nations—are presented as historical backdrop in order to understand world history. From Abraham on, the pattern is to focus on God's redemption and blessing.

The customs of Genesis often differ considerably from those of our modern day. They must be explained against their ancient Near Eastern background.

Each custom must also be treated according to the immediate context of the passage before any attempt is made to explain it based on customs recorded in extrabiblical sources or even elsewhere in Scripture.

CANAAN IN ABRAHAM'S DAY

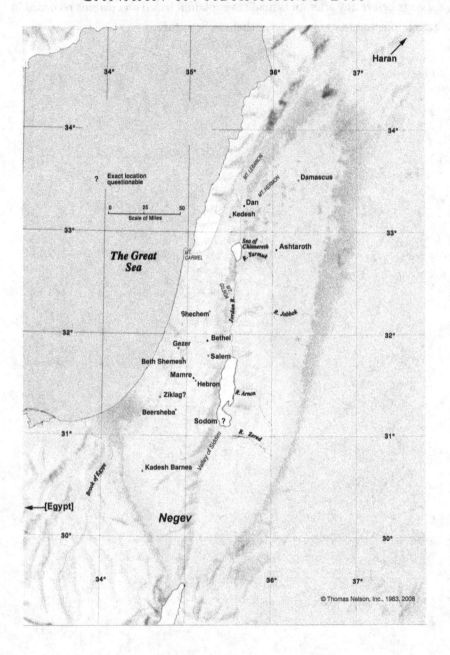

Haran

34° 35° 36° 37°

34° 34°

? Exact location
questionable

MT. LEBANON

MT. HERMON

Damascus

0 25 50
Scale of Miles

Dan
Kedesh

33° 33°

Sea of
Chinnereth

Ashtaroth

**The Great
Sea**

MT.
CARMEL

R. Yarmuk

MT.
GILBOA

Jordan R.

R. Jabbok

Shechem

32° 32°

Gezer

Bethel

Beth Shemesh

Salem

Mamre

Hebron

Ziklag?

R. Arnon

Beersheba

Sodom ?

31° 31°

R. Zered

Valley of Siddim

Kadesh Barnea

Brook of Egypt

[Egypt]

Negev

30° 30°

34° 36° 37°

1

GOD CALLS ABRAM

Genesis 12:1–20

DRAWING NEAR

The story of Abram begins with him leaving his old home and traveling to a new place that God would show him. What are some times in your life when you had to make a big move? How did it affect you and your family?

_____

_____

_____

_____

_____

THE CONTEXT

We will open our studies by meeting a man named Abram. At this point, we know very little about him. What we do know is that he is seventy-five years old, lives with his father in a place called Haran, and has a nephew named Lot.

1

However, in the coming studies, we will discover that this man is destined to become the father of the Jewish people and an important link in the family line of Jesus Himself.

The Bible introduces Abram (whose name will be changed to Abraham) by telling us that the Lord had already spoken to him in the past. God had told him to leave his father's house and travel "to a land that I will show you" (Genesis 12:1). Evidently, Abram did not know where he would be heading or what he would find when he got there. It is little wonder, in human terms, that he was hesitant to leave his family and homeland; indeed, it is a wonder that he had the faith to obey at all. Yet this is the major characteristic of the man we know as Abraham: he was a man of *faith*.

In Abram's day, many different people groups to some extent had already settled the area we know as the Middle East. As of yet, however, there was no group of people known as the Israelites or Jews. Abram himself would be the first to be called a Hebrew (meaning "one who descended from Eber"). There was also no central authority or domineering nation ruling over the region. There were, however, many fortified cities scattered around the area from Haran in the north down at least to the southerly tip of the Dead Sea, which is probably where Sodom and Gomorrah were located. The people known as the Philistines, who would one day play a major role in David's life, had already begun to settle in the area we know today as the Gaza Strip.

Traveling in this region was not like taking a road trip across the United States, where one drives on highways, eats at McDonald's, and stays at comfortable hotels. It could be a dangerous business, and one was at risk from bandits and natural hazards. People therefore traveled in groups—merchants used large caravans to carry merchandise from place to place—and such processions usually included armed guards to protect against attack. In the southern regions, water and food were not readily available, so a traveling party needed to know where they were going, how they would get there, and what supplies they would need along the way. Yet God called Abram to start walking without his extended family, without a destination, and without any guarantee except His own promise.

[**Note:** Refer to the map in the Introduction for information throughout this study.]

KEYS TO THE TEXT

Read Genesis 12:1–20, noting the key words and phrases indicated below.

> GOD'S CALL: *One day the Lord speaks to Abram, probably in a vision or dream, and commands him to leave his home and family.*

12:1. THE LORD HAD SAID: As previously noted, God had called Abram on a previous occasion and told him to leave his father's house and head south. Apparently, Abram had obeyed God partway by moving from Ur (the location of which is uncertain) to Haran—along with his father's entire household. It is worth noting that we know nothing about Abram until he began to obey. If he had continued to ignore God's call, we would probably never have heard of him—and he would not have become the father of God's chosen nation. It is characteristic of his life, however, that he obeyed God's call, as we see him beginning to do here.

ABRAM: God would not change his name to "Abraham" until after he was circumcised. The Lord did not outline His entire plan right from the beginning. Instead, He told Abram what the final outcome would be—that he would become a great nation—and then told him what the next step would require. God would reveal His plan for the next step only after Abram obeyed the immediate one.

GET OUT OF YOUR COUNTRY: Abram's first step would be to leave Haran, where he may have lived for a long time, and head south. Again, God did *not* tell him where the destination was. The command was simply, "Get out!"

TO A LAND THAT I WILL SHOW YOU: This would have seemed like a big request to Abram. With the exception of his wife, Sarai, and his nephew, Lot, Abram was to leave his family and friends behind and head to a land where he knew nobody. Along the way, he would encounter different cultures and various dangers—without knowing his final destination. We will discover, however, that this is precisely what God wanted him to experience, because Abram was destined to become a picture of God's people. Abram wandered about without making this world his home because he had his heart set on an eternal kingdom that God Himself was building (see Hebrews 11).

2. I WILL MAKE YOU A GREAT NATION: Here we find the first time that God promised to make Abram into a great nation. He was destined to be the father of the Israelites, and through him would come Messiah, Jesus the Christ,

whose death and resurrection would one day provide salvation for the entire human race. However, Abram was already seventy-five years old when God made this promise—and he had no children! This element of God's promise would prove the most difficult for Abram, and ultimately it would be the greatest test that Abram would face—especially when God called him to sacrifice his only son. But right from the beginning, Abram obeyed God and believed in His promises—even though they seemed ridiculously impossible.

3. IN YOU ALL THE FAMILIES OF THE EARTH SHALL BE BLESSED: As we will see in future studies, God's prophecies of blessing would actually begin to come true within Abram's lifetime. However, the greater fulfillment would come when God Himself entered the world through Abram's descendants in the person of Jesus Christ.

ABRAM'S OBEDIENCE: Abram obeys God's call, after some apparent delay, and leaves his home in Haran.

4. SO ABRAM DEPARTED: As we have seen, it seems to have taken Abram a while to obey God's call to leave Haran, but he eventually did. God demonstrated His patience and grace toward Abram frequently, and Abram demonstrated his own desire to please God by obeying His commands. Nevertheless, Abram was still a human being, and there were times when he fell far short of perfection.

LOT WENT WITH HIM: Lot was Abram's nephew, and he would cause real problems for Abram in the future. In fact, his presence with Abram would have an impact on the people who lived in Sodom and Gomorrah.

ABRAM WAS SEVENTY-FIVE YEARS OLD: It is true that people lived much longer in Abram's day than in modern times, yet seventy-five was still old! It was no small thing to ask a man in his mid-seventies to pack up and move away from his homeland where he had lived most of his life. Imagine how difficult it must have been for Abram to set forth on an exciting adventure at such an advanced age.

5. SARAI HIS WIFE: In the future, God would change her name to Sarah.

THE PEOPLE WHOM THEY HAD ACQUIRED IN HARAN: This probably refers to household servants rather than slaves. We will discover that Abram and Lot were wealthy and their households quite large. As we study the life of

Abram, it will be important to understand that his entourage included a great many people and large herds of livestock.

ARRIVING IN CANAAN: Abram arrives in Canaan around 2090 BC. Various groups of people (known as the Canaanites) already occupy the land.

SO THEY CAME TO THE LAND OF CANAAN: The "land of Canaan" indicates that the descendants of Canaan (Ham's son) had settled a large portion of the land that God was planning to give to Abram's descendants (see the map in this study for the route that Abram took to Canaan). Moses wrote the book of Genesis when the people of Israel—the descendants of Abram—were preparing to enter the Promised Land. The region was filled with people the Israelites would have to fight to take possession of the land, and many of these people were descended from Ham (see Genesis 9:20–25).

6. SHECHEM: Shechem is about halfway through the land of Canaan in the area known as the Fertile Crescent.

THE CANAANITES WERE THEN IN THE LAND: Put yourself in Abram's place. God has called you to travel to an undefined location, with the understanding that He is going to give you many descendants and make your family into a great nation. But when you arrive, you find that the land is already populated—by people who are likely to be hostile to you! Most people would have balked at this point and wondered whether they had made a mistake. However, Abram stepped out in faith, and God faithfully honored him for it.

GOD ENCOURAGES ABRAM'S FAITH: Abram had obeyed God's command to leave Haran. Now the Lord comes to him to encourage his faith—and to tell him something new.

7. THEN THE LORD APPEARED TO ABRAM: At this point, God bolstered Abram's faith by reiterating His promise—and by adding some new information to it. In the future, the Lord would appear often to Abram to reiterate His promise and reveal new details—but only *after* Abram obeyed what he had been told to do. Here, Abram had finally obeyed God's command to travel to Canaan, so God encouraged his faith.

5

TO YOUR DESCENDANTS I WILL GIVE THIS LAND: This is a new piece of information. Prior to this, God had only told Abram that he would become a great nation, but here God told Abram that his descendants would inherit the entire land of Canaan. God was encouraging Abram to trust Him at His word, despite appearances and circumstances. Even though the land was already settled and populated, God insisted that He would one day give the entire land to Abram's descendants. Circumstances made that promise seem impossible, yet Abram continued to place his faith in God's word.

HE BUILT AN ALTAR TO THE LORD: This act demonstrates that Abram chose to believe God even when His promise seemed impossible. Everywhere Abram traveled, he built altars to the Lord and proclaimed His name to the people around him.

8. HE MOVED FROM THERE: Abram's life would be characterized by his constant moving from one place to another. He was to never settle permanently in any one location, and he would spend the remainder of his days living in tents rather than in a permanent house. (It is likely that he and his family lived in houses, rather than tents, when they were in Haran.)

CALLED ON THE NAME OF THE LORD: The Hebrew word translated "called" means "to cry out" or "to proclaim." Abram worshiped God in a public manner, proclaiming His character to the people around him. Remember that there were many people traveling with Abram as part of his household, and there were many traveling in Lot's household as well. In proclaiming God publicly, Abram was already beginning to fulfill his role as a blessing to the nations.

> FAMINE: *Abram has been wandering about in the land of Canaan, living in a tent and pasturing his flocks. Then along comes trouble . . .*

10. THERE WAS A FAMINE IN THE LAND: Famine and the land of Egypt figured prominently in the history of Israel, right up to the time of their exodus from Egypt. God uses the circumstances of our lives—both the good and the bad, the blessings and the trials—to lead us in His will. This particular famine would lead Abram to a time of testing in Egypt, just as it would someday lead to a time of blessing in Egypt for Abram's descendants (see Genesis 47:27).

FEAR: Abram begins to fear what will happen to him in Egypt, and he talks himself into fearing the worst. This lack of trust will end up having long-term consequences for him, his family, and the world as a whole.

11. YOU ARE A WOMAN OF BEAUTIFUL COUNTENANCE: Sarai was sixty-five when Abram (aged seventy-five) left Haran. It is unclear how much time had passed, but she was at least in her late sixties.

12. IT WILL HAPPEN: Here we see Abram struggling with a lack of faith in God's promises. He had convinced himself in fear that bad things were going to happen—though they never did. Fear leads God's people into doubt, not faith. The Lord Himself commands us frequently in the Bible to "be of good courage" and "fear not."

THEY WILL KILL ME: Abram was made of the same flesh that we are, which is encouraging news. Here he lapsed from his great faith in God's promises. If he had clung to them, he would have realized that the Egyptians *couldn't* kill him, because he was destined to become a great nation—even though he didn't have any children yet. His own logic could have reassured him that he had to live at least long enough to have offspring, but fear blinded both his logic and faith.

13. SAY YOU ARE MY SISTER: This was partially true, for Sarai was actually Abram's half sister; they shared the same father but different mothers. Nevertheless, a half-truth is still a lie, and it got Abram and his wife into trouble—more than once! What is worse, Abram was encouraging his wife— and probably the rest of his household—to sin.

15. THE WOMAN WAS TAKEN TO PHARAOH'S HOUSE: This statement is loaded with significance because it implies that Abram did nothing to prevent it. Abram had effectively allowed another man to take his wife, with the intention of making her part of his harem. Fear had driven Abram so far from being a man of faith that he had sold out his own wife.

HE TREATED ABRAM WELL FOR HER SAKE: Now we discover that Abram was even making a *profit* from the situation, like a pimp with his prostitute. This is a low point in Abram's walk with God.

MALE AND FEMALE SERVANTS: Pharaoh gave Abram many gifts, including "male and female servants." It is quite possible that Hagar was one of these female servants. She would bring further trouble to Abram in the future.

God Intervenes: Abram's lack of faith actually endangers God's plans for the coming Messiah. But God will not permit man's actions to interfere with His plans.

17. **The Lord plagued Pharaoh and his house with great plagues because of Sarai**: The significance of Abram's action is much deeper than lying about his wife. God intended to bring His Redeemer through Abram's seed, and He would later make it clear that He meant to bring about His chosen people (and His Chosen One) through the offspring of Abram and Sarai. Yet here was Abram offering his wife to another man, with the very real possibility that Sarai would have that man's child. For this reason—and because Sarai was the one in real peril from a human perspective—God intervened to protect her from becoming one of Pharaoh's wives.

18. **What is this you have done to me**: Abram's lack of faith also placed Pharaoh and his entire household in jeopardy. It is a principle of sin that one man's sin will often endanger many others. What's worse, Pharaoh had not done anything to threaten Abram; indeed, he had been generous in giving him gifts. The whole problem arose because Abram was afraid and failed to place his trust in God's protection. Alas, this entire sad episode would be repeated when Abraham met Abimelech, another king (see Genesis 20).

THE JOURNEYS OF ABRAM

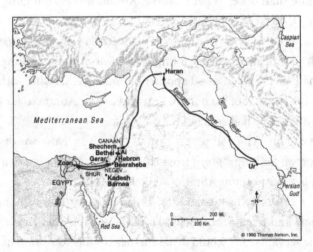

UNLEASHING THE TEXT

1) If you had been in Abram's place, how would you have responded to God's command to leave your home and family?

_____

_____

_____

_____

_____

2) What were the costs to Abram to obey God's call?

_____

_____

_____

_____

_____

3) When have you been called to make a radical change in your own life for God? What were the costs? The results?

_____

_____

_____

_____

_____

4) Why did Abram lie to Pharaoh? How do you think it made Sarai feel? How might you have responded if you were in Pharaoh's place?

_____

_____

_____

_____

_____

_____

EXPLORING THE MEANING

God calls His people to walk in faith. God revealed a small portion of His plan to Abram, and then He asked Abram to respond by walking away from all that he knew as home and family. In fact, He asked Abram to walk into a strange land without even knowing exactly where he was going or what he would find when he got there.

This is what it means to walk in faith: to step into the unknown, even into threatening circumstances, with only God's word to depend on. Abram arrived in Canaan to find himself surrounded with unfriendly people, and then God told him that he would inherit the entire land for his descendants. Circumstances made this seem impossible, yet Abram believed God and took Him at His word. He was seventy-five years old and had no children, yet he believed that God was going to give him many descendants.

Walking in faith requires that we accept God's Word at face value, even when it seems impossible that His promises can come true. In this, Abram and Sarai provide us with a great role model.

Often God will not reveal the next step until we obey the present step. Abram understood only that he would have children and that those children would become a great nation. He did not know where they would live or how such things could be accomplished—all he knew was that God wanted him to leave Haran and move to Canaan. It was not until he arrived in Canaan that God told him the next part of His plan: to give his descendants the entire land of Canaan as their home.

The truth is that God's plan for Abram's descendants went way beyond acquiring the Promised Land and becoming a great nation. Ultimately, God was planning to bring forth His Messiah, His Son Jesus, through the descendants of Abram. Abram did not know any of these details, yet God expected him to obey just the same.

God expects His children today to live the same way. He does not always reveal to us the fullness of His plans for our lives and the lives of those we influence. Instead, He tells us what we need to know in order to obey Him one step at a time. To discover the next step in His plan, we must first obey the present step.

Fear is the enemy of God's people. Fear is what led Abram to make a disastrous blunder in Egypt. Fear would lead him to make the *same exact mistake* later. He became afraid of the unknown in Egypt, even after he had trusted God with the great unknown of Canaan. Had he reminded himself of God's faithfulness and God's promise that he would become a great nation, Abram might have conquered his fear and continued to live by faith.

Satan loves to use fear to draw God's people out of obedience. When this happens, they are tempted to take matters into their own hands. Abram certainly did this when he devised what he thought was a clever plan to avoid being killed, and the results were bad and far-reaching. Today, the Evil One uses fear—of the future, the past, and the present—to mislead us in the same way so that our choices also reap results that are negative and far-reaching. When anxiety creeps in, we are wise to remind ourselves of all that God has done for us already and to focus our minds on His promises. God's Word drives out the Devil's fears.

REFLECTING ON THE TEXT

5) Why did God call Abram to leave Haran in the first place? Why did He call Abram to leave his father's household? Why couldn't Abram just stay where he was?

_____

_____

_____

_____

6) Why does God often reveal His will one step at a time? Why does He not give us a clear outline of all that He has planned?

_____

_____

_____

_____

7) In what ways did God lead Abram in Genesis 12? How does He lead His people today?

_____

_____

_____

_____

_____

8) How does Satan use fear to lead people away from God?

_____

_____

_____

_____

PERSONAL RESPONSE

9) What step of obedience is God asking of you today? What is it going to cost you?

_____

_____

_____

_____

10) What fears are you facing? What circumstances or "unknowns" are taking your eyes off of trusting God? What Scriptures can help you place your trust back in God's faithfulness?

_____

_____

_____

_____

2

DEALING WITH LOT
Genesis 13:1–14:17

DRAWING NEAR

In today's reading, Abram's nephew Lot made a choice that he thought would turn out good but ended up being very bad. Recall a time when you chose something that seemed good in the moment but ended up with negative consequences in the long run.

_____

_____

_____

_____

THE CONTEXT

In the last study, we took a brief look at the events that occurred during Abram's time in Egypt. Genesis 13 begins with Abram and his household leaving that country. His nephew Lot is still with him.

As our passage opens, Abram and Lot are standing on a high mountainous area, looking out over all of Canaan. Below them, to the east, was one of the few truly level areas in Canaan—a fertile valley watered by the Jordan River. Not far to the south, at the mouth of that valley, lay what we call today the Dead Sea or the Salt Sea. When Abram and Lot looked out on that sea, however, it appeared very different than it does now—if it existed at all. Where the southern end of the Dead Sea lies today, Abram and Lot looked on several thriving and prosperous cities, including Sodom and Gomorrah.

Lot would now separate from Abram, and evidently he would continue to live as a nomad for a time. As he traveled, however, he moved closer and closer to the city of Sodom, eventually giving up his nomadic ways and settling into a comfortable urban lifestyle. This choice came with an immediate price when the cities of Sodom and Gomorrah rebelled against their overlord. Lot was carried into captivity, forcing Abram to come to his rescue, yet even then he did not desert the city. In fact, when we meet him again, he will be sitting in the seat of a city elder, acting as a significant leader in Sodom. Lot will have walked, stood, and finally sat down with the wicked.

KEYS TO THE TEXT

Read Genesis 13:1–14:17, noting the key words and phrases indicated below.

> LEAVING EGYPT: *As our passage opens, Abram has finished his time in Egypt and is now heading north into Canaan. He will ultimately stop at Bethel.*

13:1. ABRAM WENT UP FROM EGYPT: As you will recall from the last study, Abram had been staying in Egypt, and during this time he had told Pharaoh that his wife, Sarai, was only his sister (see Genesis 12 for more information).

AND LOT WITH HIM: Abram's nephew Lot traveled with him, as he had done since the pair left Haran.

TO THE SOUTH: Abram and company were not traveling southward; they were actually heading northeast toward Canaan. However, they were entering the southern section of Canaan, which was known as the Negev. The sense here is that they traveled to the southern sections of Canaan.

2. ABRAM WAS VERY RICH: Abram also had a great many people traveling with him in his household, as we will see. Lot evidently had similar wealth.

3. BETHEL: Bethel is located in the hills overlooking the Jordan River valley, which was the most level and fertile area in Canaan. (See the map in the Introduction.)

4. ABRAM CALLED ON THE NAME OF THE LORD: Once again, we see this man of God depending on God in his daily life. This was the pattern wherever Abram went.

TOO MUCH STUFF: Because of Abram and Lot's great wealth, the land can no longer support them both. This wealth will prove to be a trap for Lot.

5. LOT ... HAD FLOCKS AND HERDS AND TENTS: Like Abram, Lot probably had numerous servants and hired hands. Each of these people likely had a family, tent, and household possessions, and many probably had livestock of their own.

6. THE LAND WAS NOT ABLE TO SUPPORT THEM: A conservative estimate of Abram's traveling household would be at least one thousand people. He also had flocks of sheep and herds of cattle, and the people who worked for him almost certainly had possessions of their own. Add to this the household of Lot, and we realize that Abram had an enormous amount of people moving about with him. It would have been difficult for him to navigate such a large group, and finding suitable grazing and living space would have been a logistical nightmare.

THEIR POSSESSIONS WERE SO GREAT THAT THEY COULD NOT DWELL TOGETHER: Due to the extent of their wealth, it was no longer possible for Abram and Lot to continue traveling together. Here is a tragic fact of our world—even close kin are driven apart by possessions. We are told, however, that Abram's focus was on the things of eternity rather than the things of this temporal world (see Hebrews 11:9–10). Lot, on the other hand, was more interested in temporal gain. His selfish choices would eventually lead him to Sodom and, consequently, into great spiritual peril.

7. THE CANAANITES AND THE PERIZZITES THEN DWELT IN THE LAND: This is an odd statement to follow the fact that Abram's herdsmen were fighting with Lot's herdsmen. The implication, however, is that the world around Abram was watching, and his strife with Lot was producing a poor testimony.

*PARTING COMPANY AT LAST: After years of traveling together,
Abram and Lot part company. Abram's path will be marked by
divine protection, while Lot's will be characterized by temptation
and compromise.*

9. PLEASE SEPARATE FROM ME: After having dwelt together for so long,
Abram separated from Lot more by compulsion than by choice. Yet God was
using these circumstances to providentially divide the two—and send Abram
in the opposite direction from the evil influences of Sodom and Gomorrah.

IF YOU TAKE THE LEFT, THEN I WILL GO TO THE RIGHT: Abram here
demonstrated great humility and generosity. By every standard, he had the
perfect right to choose for himself first: he was older, he was Lot's uncle, he was
head of the household, and so forth. Yet he deferred to his nephew and allowed
him to choose where to settle.

10. LOT LIFTED HIS EYES: This interesting phrase appears frequently in
Genesis. It is worthwhile to take note in each case of what the person saw when
he lifted his eyes, because this gives insight into what was in that person's heart.
In this case, Lot lifted his eyes and saw what he most wanted: choice land and
wealth.

THE PLAIN OF JORDAN: This is the valley where the Jordan River flows,
running between the Dead Sea (or Salt Sea) and the Sea of Galilee. This area is
fertile and flat, which are two important qualities in the land of Canaan. This
would have been equivalent to the choicest and most expensive real estate in
the entire region. Lot's eye fell on the area where the wealthy dwelled.

BEFORE THE LORD DESTROYED SODOM AND GOMORRAH: It is quite
possible that the Dead Sea did not exist or was substantially smaller at this
point in history. Sodom probably stood at the south end of what is now the
Dead Sea.

*LOT's CHOICE: Lot looks out on the fertile Jordan River valley
below him, and wealth and comfort beckon to him. He will follow
this desire all the way to Sodom.*

11. LOT CHOSE FOR HIMSELF: Abram had just shown great deference toward Lot, and the proper response would have been for Lot to return it back to

his uncle, insisting that Abram choose first—as was his right. Instead, Lot chose for himself, looking out for his own interests and satisfying his own desires.

12. ABRAM DWELT IN THE LAND OF CANAAN: In tents, as we have noted previously. This was in stark contrast to the future urban lifestyle of his nephew.

LOT DWELT IN THE CITIES OF THE PLAIN: The cities of Canaan (and beyond) represented a constant threat in the life of Abram. Whenever he went to the city, trouble followed. This pattern also held true for his nephew Lot. The cities of the plain were probably fortified with large walls and standing armies. They were without doubt wealthy and comfortable, but they were also characterized by great wickedness.

PITCHED HIS TENT EVEN AS FAR AS SODOM: This is probably a figure of speech in this instance, as we discover Lot living in a house inside the walls of Sodom. It is possible, however, that he remained a nomad for a time after leaving Abram and gradually moved south until he came to Sodom, where he settled permanently—or so he thought. The allure of worldly pleasures and comfort frequently work this way, moving us a little at a time until one day we find ourselves entrenched in the world's system.

13. THE MEN OF SODOM WERE EXCEEDINGLY WICKED: Lot would have known that the people of Sodom were wicked before he even moved into that city. Lot himself was a righteous man, as the New Testament testifies (see 2 Peter 2:7), and one would think he would have been unwilling to live in a city that was renowned for its wickedness. Yet this only serves to demonstrate the deadly power that wealth and comfort can exert on us—even on those who belong to the family of God.

> PROMISE OF LAND: Now that Abram has parted company
> with his nephew Lot, God is ready to appear to him with further
> information concerning His promise.

14. THE PLACE WHERE YOU ARE: Abram was encamped near Bethel, which is roughly at the center of the area that would come to be known as Palestine.

15. ALL THE LAND: The land of Canaan. Remember that Moses wrote the book of Genesis during the time when the Israelites were wandering in

the wilderness, and perhaps just prior to the time when they would enter the land of Canaan and claim it as their own. However, the Israelites had already surveyed the Promised Land on a previous occasion and discovered that the people who dwelled there were "strong" and that their cities were "fortified and very large" (Numbers 13:28).

I GIVE TO YOU AND YOUR DESCENDANTS FOREVER: It was important for the Israelites to understand *why* they were claiming the Promised Land, because they had lost heart on the verge of entering it. Moses reminded them in this passage that God had promised Canaan to Abram's descendants, and they could therefore trust Him to protect them as they entered it.

> PROMISE OF DESCENDANTS: *God has already promised to Abram that he will have children, but here He reveals that Abram's descendants will be innumerable.*

16. I WILL MAKE YOUR DESCENDANTS AS THE DUST OF THE EARTH: This promise was fulfilled literally in the physical descendants of Abram. In Solomon's day, "Judah and Israel were as numerous as the sand by the sea in multitude" (1 Kings 4:20). Yet it is also fulfilled to an even greater extent when we add in the countless multitudes that have accepted Christ and, spiritually speaking, become "the seed of Abraham." In Galatians 3:29, the apostle Paul says, "And if you are Christ's, then you are Abraham's seed, and heirs according to the promise."

18. ABRAM MOVED HIS TENT: This, as we have seen, was the pattern for the remainder of Abram's life: he never stayed in one place for an extended length of time. Genesis reminds us of his unsettled life repeatedly, and the New Testament tells us that Abraham is an example for God's people to follow. We are called to be "strangers and pilgrims on the earth" (Hebrews 11:13), always focusing our eyes on eternity.

BUILT AN ALTAR THERE TO THE LORD: This, too, was a pattern in Abram's life: wherever he went, he built an altar and called on the name of the Lord. Building an altar in Abram's culture was a public statement of what god a person worshiped. Abram's household consisted of a great many people, so when he built an altar and offered a sacrifice, he was leading many hundreds of people—perhaps more than a thousand—in worshiping the Lord.

LOT'S CAPTURE: Lot finds his choice of residence in Sodom has led to the first of many negative consequences to come.

14:4. IN THE THIRTEENTH YEAR THEY REBELLED: Raiding, conquering, and making other kings and city-states subservient vassals were all part of the world of the Fertile Crescent in Abraham's day. When vassal states thought they could throw off the yoke of their conquerors, they rebelled by not paying the assessed tribute and waited for any military response.

5. IN THE FOURTEENTH YEAR CHEDORLAOMER AND THE KINGS THAT WERE WITH HIM ATTACKED: This time, the vassal states' rebellion evoked a major military response by Chedorlaomer and his allies. Sodom and Gomorrah lost, and Lot, by then a resident of Sodom, was taken captive.

10. VALLEY OF SIDDIM: Perhaps this was the large peninsula that comes out into the Dead Sea from the eastern shore. In Abram's time, it may have come all the way across to the western shore (near Masada), so the southern one-third of the current Dead Sea formed this dry valley.

13. ONE WHO HAD ESCAPED: One of the survivors fled from the invaders and located Lot's uncle. One as wealthy as Abram would not be hard to find, and obviously they thought he could do something about the crisis.

THE HEBREW: For the first time in the biblical record, this ethnic appellation, "descended from Eber," is accorded to Abram. Foreigners used it of Israelites, and Israelites used it of themselves in the presence of foreigners.

LOT'S RESCUE: When Abram hears of Lot's capture, he immediately gathers his forces to go in pursuit of his nephew.

14. TRAINED SERVANTS: Abram's private militia—318 members of his extended family—were highly skilled bodyguards and the protective force for his possessions. Abram mustered this force, along with the trained men of his allies, and set off in pursuit of the military kidnappers to prevent captives from being taken away to the east, to Shinar (the early name for Mesopotamia) or further east, to Elam.

15. HIS SERVANTS ATTACKED THEM AND PURSUED THEM: A battle-wise Abram, no stranger to military strategy, pursued the enemy for more than 150 miles and defeated the marauding consortium.

17. THE VALLEY OF SHAVEH: The liberated king of Sodom went to meet Abram near Jerusalem.

UNLEASHING THE TEXT

1) When Abram and Lot separated, why did Lot choose to go down into the valley? What does this show about his priorities?

_____

_____

_____

_____

_____

2) How did Abram's choices affect others? How did Lot's? Give specific examples.

_____

_____

_____

_____

_____

3) In what ways did God orchestrate this separation? Why was it necessary for this to happen for God to reveal His next steps to Abram?

_____

_____

_____

_____

_____

4) What were the immediate results of Lot's choice to live in Sodom? How did it affect his family? How did it affect Abram?

_____

_____

_____

_____

EXPLORING THE MEANING

Our actions have far-reaching impact in the lives of others. Abram and Lot made different decisions about where to live and what lifestyle to adopt, and those decisions influenced both of their families—and the entire nation of Israel—for hundreds of years to come.

This is a principle that we find reiterated throughout Scripture: our obedience or disobedience will affect the lives of others in ways that we cannot foresee. The ultimate example of this, of course, is in the life of the Lord Himself, whose complete and perfect obedience to the Father's will affected the lives of every person who has ever lived—and who ever will.

It is easy sometimes to think that some little point of disobedience or some small indulgence in sin will be harmless—"just this once." But we do not know what long-ranging impact that compromising decision may have in the lives of others.

The comforts of the world can become a deadly trap. Lot did not leave Abram and head straight for a new house in Sodom—he arrived there by degrees. So it is with the comforts and entanglements of the world: they grow on us a little at a time.

This is a difficult balance, because the Lord's people are called to be in the world but not of the world. We have no choice but to live in society and take part in the workaday economy, yet we must also be on guard to ensure that these entanglements do not become the focus of our lives.

"Do not love the world or the things in the world. If anyone loves the world, the love of the Father is not in him. For all that is in the world—the lust of the flesh, the lust of the eyes, and the pride of life—is not of the Father but is of the world. And the world is passing away, and the lust of it; but he who does the will of God abides forever" (1 John 2:15–17).

Associating with evil leads to negative consequences. By the time Chedorlaomer decided to put down the rebellion in his vassal territories, Lot was firmly enmeshed in the community at Sodom. When the cities fell, his goods were confiscated, and he was taken captive along with the others. Lot, by simply being in the wrong place at the wrong time, paid the price for the wicked kings' decision to rebel.

In 1 Corinthians 5:11, Paul warns us to not "keep company with anyone named a brother, who is sexually immoral, or covetous, or an idolater, or a reviler, or a drunkard, or an extortioner—not even to eat with such a person." It was Lot's greed that led him to select the choicest plot of land in Canaan. In turn, this led to him associating with evil, which led to him getting caught up in the cities' rebellion.

We may think that our choice in friends or relationships will not have any impact on our lives, but "evil company corrupts good habits" (1 Corinthians 15:33). Like Lot, we may find one day that our compromises have led us to a place that we never intended to be. Even then, God is merciful and will rescue us when we call out to Him, but we can avoid a lot of pain in the first place if we simply avoid evil.

REFLECTING ON THE TEXT

5) What further promise did God make to Abram once he had parted from Lot? Why was it important for Moses to remind the Israelites of this promise?

_____

_____

_____

_____

6) In what ways was Abram's life characterized by an attitude of worship? What did his pattern of building altars to God reveal to those around him?

_____

_____

_____

_____

_____

7) How did Lot get caught up in the struggle between Chedorlaomer and his vassal states? How might he have avoided this conflict?

_____

_____

_____

_____

_____

8) In what ways would it have been easy for Abram to be bitter about Lot's choice of land? What does it say about his character that he immediately went to his nephew's aid when Lot was in trouble?

_____

_____

_____

_____

_____

PERSONAL RESPONSE

9) In what ways have you made subtle compromises with evil? What do you
   feel God is asking you to do to break those ties?

_____

_____

_____

_____

10) In what ways have you allowed bitterness to keep you from helping others?
    How can you be more like Abram and help those in crisis?

_____

_____

_____

_____

3

THE PROMISE TO ABRAM
Genesis 15:1–21

DRAWING NEAR

Abram, unlike his nephew Lot, spent most of his days moving from place to place. What are some of the advantages of living such a semi-nomadic life? What are some of the disadvantages?

_____

_____

_____

_____

THE CONTEXT

Abram was now living in Canaan, moving from place to place, dwelling in tents. From a human perspective, there was no reason for him to not settle in one location, build permanent structures, fortify the area with a large wall—and even establish a small standing army. Had he done that, Abram would have been just like his neighbors. Those neighbors might have been uncomfortable to have a man of such great wealth establish yet another stronghold in their region, but in time everyone might have adjusted. This was the age of great

27

empires, such as Egypt, which flourished with majestic architecture, art, and politics. Even smaller city-states were fortified with surrounding walls, heavy gates, and well-trained armies.

Much of Canaan consisted of the area known as the Fertile Crescent, an arc of land today that is well watered and productive. If you look at the map in study 1, the arrows showing Abraham's journeys roughly define the Fertile Crescent, arcing from Ur down to Beersheba. The area south of Beersheba, called the Negev, is much more arid and rocky. This region is suitable for grazing flocks in the winter season, but shepherds must move their flocks north for pasture during other times of the year.

This lifestyle is the one that Abram—unlike his nephew Lot—chose rather than settling himself inside of solid city walls. He spent the remainder of his life as a nomad, moving from place to place and pasturing his flocks where there was food, as dictated by the seasons. Again, this is not normal behavior for a man of great wealth and power (he actually defeated the armies of four kings—see Genesis 14). In order to understand his motives, we must look more closely at the promise from God, for it was on this promise that Abram was making his decisions and building for his future.

KEYS TO THE TEXT

Read Genesis 15:1–21, noting the key words and phrases indicated below.

> GOD PROMISES HIMSELF: *God has just promised that Abram's descendants will be innumerable (see Genesis 13:14–16). Now He will reveal the greatest detail of all His promises: He Himself will be Abram's "exceedingly great reward" (Genesis 15:1).*

15:1. DO NOT BE AFRAID, ABRAM: We will soon discover that Abram was afraid that God's promises could not come true—at least, not without his help. We already saw this in the passages from study 1, and we will see it carried even further when Abram attempts to sire a son through his wife's maid, Hagar. Fear leads people to move away from faith rather than toward it.

I AM YOUR ... EXCEEDINGLY GREAT REWARD: This was the very core of God's promises to Abram and to his descendants—God was promising

Himself, not merely many descendants and a nice piece of real estate. Abram's descendants would be the ones to bring forth the Messiah, God's only Son, and through Him the entire human race would regain access into the presence of God.

ABRAM NEEDS REASSURANCE: Despite all of God's personal appearances to Abram, he is still unsure that the promises will come to pass.

2. WHAT WILL YOU GIVE ME: This was a rather bold question for a sinful man to pose to the almighty God. It was almost as if Abram were demanding some proof that God would keep His word. God had already visited Abram several times and reiterated His promise of an heir and a home. Abram had done nothing to deserve this promise—God did not owe him anything. Nevertheless, God here demonstrated His great mercy and patience by honoring Abram's request.

THE HEIR OF MY HOUSE IS ELIEZER OF DAMASCUS: To Abram, God's promise had stalled; so adoption of a servant as the male heir—a well-known contemporary Mesopotamian custom—was the best officially recognizable arrangement to make it come to pass, humanly speaking.

3. YOU HAVE GIVEN ME NO OFFSPRING: Abram's question, "What will You give me?" (Genesis 15:2) became an accusation: "You have given me no offspring." It had been years since God first appeared to Abram and promised him descendants, and yet no son had been born. We need to remember that Abram was only a man, and even a man of great faith will need some encouragement from time to time if he is to hold firm to trusting God's word.

4. THIS ONE SHALL NOT BE YOUR HEIR: That is, the man named Eliezer of Damascus (see Genesis 15:2).

ONE WHO WILL COME FROM YOUR OWN BODY SHALL BE YOUR HEIR: Abram would later take this promise in the narrowest interpretation, allowing his wife to persuade him to have a child with one of his servants. God would make it more abundantly clear to Abram in the future that his heir would come not only from his own body but from his wife's own body too. The difficulty for Abram was that he was at least eighty years old by this time, and his wife at least seventy. God was asking Abram to place his faith in something that was completely impossible.

> ABRAM'S RIGHTEOUSNESS: *Abram believes God's word—even before the Lord has sealed the covenant in ritual fashion—and God counts this as righteousness.*

6. HE BELIEVED IN THE LORD: We will consider this important verse in more detail in study 6, but for now it is important to recognize that this was at the core of Abram's character: he believed God. God was asking him to believe in something that was utterly impossible, and his own eyes told him that the promise hadn't come true for years already. Abram had no guarantee to bank on other than God's word, but he still chose to believe in the Lord.

HE ACCOUNTED IT TO HIM FOR RIGHTEOUSNESS: Abram was the "father of our faith," and as Christians we are called "sons of Abraham." The reason for this high honor is that Abram demonstrated *faith*, which is the basic ingredient of being reconciled with God. The New Testament uses Abram as an example of those who are saved by faith in Jesus Christ. "Now it was not written for [Abram's] sake alone that it was imputed to him, but also for us. It shall be imputed to us who believe in Him who raised up Jesus our Lord from the dead, who was delivered up because of our offenses, and was raised because of our justification" (Romans 4:23–25).

> THE COVENANT: *God has Abram set out his culture's equivalent of a legal contract. By performing this ritual, God binds Himself to fulfill His promise.*

8. HOW SHALL I KNOW THAT I WILL INHERIT IT: This time, Abram's question was not a veiled accusation at the delayed fulfillment of God's promise but a genuine request for information and assurance. In response, God affirmed His covenant with Abram through a remarkable ceremony.

9. BRING ME A THREE-YEAR-OLD HEIFER: In giving this instruction, God was beginning the ceremony. This would be an unconditional covenant, which meant that God committed Himself to fulfill it regardless of what Abram did—no commitment was required of Abram for the covenant

to be valid. The animals that God commanded Abram to sacrifice in this covenant were the same ones He would later include in the law that He revealed to Moses. The laws of sacrifices were complex and demanding, but the one thing that remained consistent throughout the entire law was that without the shedding of blood, there could be no remission of sins (see Hebrews 9:22).

10. CUT THEM IN TWO: Ancient covenants often involved this form of animal sacrifice. An animal was cut in half, and the two parties to the covenant walked between them. This was a symbolic way of saying, "May the same happen to me if I do not keep this covenant" (see Jeremiah 34:18–19).

12. A DEEP SLEEP FELL UPON ABRAM: We are not specifically told how God appeared to Abram in each instance, but it appears that up to this point He only came to him in dreams or visions. God did appear in person before Abraham later, but only after he was circumcised.

PROPHECIES OF THE FUTURE: *God now reveals to Abram some of His plan for the future of his descendants. These prophecies foretell Israel's captivity and escape from Egypt.*

13. YOUR DESCENDANTS WILL BE STRANGERS: The Israelites would eventually serve as slaves in Egypt for 430 years before God brought them out under the leadership of Moses. Remember that Moses himself was writing Genesis during that very exodus. These historical passages undoubtedly helped the Israelites find encouragement during their wanderings in the wilderness.

14. THE NATION WHOM THEY SERVE I WILL JUDGE: God would send plagues on Egypt to force Pharaoh to release the Israelites, and He would finally destroy the Egyptian army when it pursued His people into the wilderness.

THEY SHALL COME OUT WITH GREAT POSSESSIONS: God directed the Israelites to "spoil the Egyptians" before leaving (see Exodus 11:2).

15. A GOOD OLD AGE: Abraham lived to be 175 (see Genesis 25:7).

THE INIQUITY OF THE AMORITES IS NOT YET COMPLETE: God demonstrated His mercy and patience repeatedly in the book of Genesis, offering men many opportunities to repent and find salvation. But the time did come when a man's—and a nation's—stubborn wickedness reached its full measure. At that point, the justice of God fell. Once the iniquity of the Canaanites (broadly de-fined ethnically as the Amorites) reached its full measure, God would send His people into the land to eradicate them.

17. A SMOKING OVEN AND A BURNING TORCH: These items symbol-ized the presence of God, who solemnly promised by divine oath to fulfill His word to Abram. Old Testament manifestations of God's presence frequently emphasized His justice and power. In this case, the oven and torch could sug-gest God's burning zeal and His potential wrath.

PASSED BETWEEN THOSE PIECES: It is interesting to note that Abram never passed between the sacrificed animals—only God passed through. This is because Abram had no part in the fulfillment of this covenant—God would make good on His promises to Abram regardless of the future actions of Abram and his descendants.

GOING DEEPER

Read Romans 4:1–25, noting the key words and phrases indicated below.

> JUSTIFIED BY FAITH: *In his letter to the Romans, Paul uses this story of Abraham show how it is faith, not works, that justifies us before God.*

4:1. ABRAHAM, OUR FOREFATHER: Paul used the model of Abraham to prove justification by faith alone because the Jews held him up as the supreme example of a righteous man (see John 8:39), and because it clearly showed that Judaism with its works-righteousness had deviated from the faith of the Jews' patriarchal ancestors.

3. ABRAHAM BELIEVED GOD: This quotation from Genesis 15:6 is one of the clearest statements in all Scripture about justification. Used in both financial and legal settings, this Greek word, which occurs nine times in Ro-mans 4 alone, means to take something that belongs to someone and credit it to another's account. It is a one-sided transaction—Abraham did nothing to accumulate it; God simply credited it to him. God took His own righteous-ness and credited it to Abraham as if it were his simply because Abraham believed in Him.

4. TO HIM WHO WORKS: Broadening his argument from Abraham to all people, Paul makes it clear that the act of declaring a person righteous is completely separate from any kind of human work.

JUSTIFIED BEFORE CIRCUMCISION: Paul explains why, if Abraham was justified by faith alone, God commanded him and his descendants to be circumcised.

9. DOES THIS BLESSEDNESS THEN COME UPON THE CIRCUMCISED ONLY: Paul here anticipates what his Jewish readers would be thinking: *If Abraham was justified by his faith alone, why did God command him and his descendants to be circumcised?* Paul's response not only answers those concerned with circumcision but also those who cling to some other kind of religious ceremony or activity as their basis for righteousness.

10. NOT WHILE CIRCUMCISED, BUT WHILE UNCIRCUMCISED: The chronology of Genesis proves Paul's case. Abraham was ninety-nine when he was circumcised, but God had already declared him righteous at least fourteen years before.

11. THE FATHER OF ALL THOSE WHO BELIEVE: Racially, Abraham was the father of all Jews (circumcised); spiritually, he was the father of both believing Jews and believing Gentiles (uncircumcised).

NOT JUSTIFIED THROUGH THE LAW: Paul explains that in the same way Abraham was not justified by the rite of circumcision, neither was he justified by keeping the Mosaic Law.

13. PROMISE THAT HE WOULD BE THE HEIR OF THE WORLD: This refers to Christ and is the essence of the covenant God made with Abraham and his descendants. The final provision of that covenant was that through Abraham's seed all the world would be blessed (see Genesis 12:3). All believers, by being in Christ, become heirs of the promise.

NOT ... THROUGH THE LAW: That is, not as a result of Abraham's keeping the law.

14. THOSE WHO ARE OF THE LAW: If only those who perfectly keep the law (an impossibility) receive the promise, then faith has no value.

PROMISE MADE OF NO EFFECT: Making a promise contingent on an impossible condition nullifies the promise.

16. IT IS OF FAITH THAT IT MIGHT BE ACCORDING TO GRACE: Justification comes through faith alone, but the power of justification comes through God's great grace, not man's faith.

17. CALLS THOSE THINGS WHICH DO NOT EXIST AS THOUGH THEY DID: This is another reference to the forensic nature of justification. God can declare believing sinners to be righteous, even though they are not, by imputing His righteousness to them—just as God made or declared Jesus "sin" and punished Him, though He was not a sinner. Those whom God justifies, He will conform to the image of His Son.

JUSTIFICATION FROM GOD: *Paul now concludes by showing that justification results from divine power, not from human effort.*

18. CONTRARY TO HOPE: Paul here is referring to the fact that from a human perspective, it seemed impossible for Abraham to become a father of many nations.

DEADNESS OF SARAH'S WOMB: Remember that Sarah was only ten years younger than Abraham. She was ninety years old and well past childbearing age when they received the promise of Isaac (see Genesis 17:17).

20. THE PROMISE: Of the birth of a son (see Genesis 15:4; 17:16; 18:10).

GIVING GLORY TO GOD: Believing God affirms His existence and character and thus gives Him glory.

22. THEREFORE "IT WAS ACCOUNTED TO HIM": Paul concludes by reiterating that it was because of Abraham's genuine *faith* that God credited him with righteousness.

23. NOT WRITTEN FOR HIS SAKE ALONE: All Scripture has universal application, and Abraham's experience is no exception. If Abraham was justified by faith, then all other people are justified on the same basis.

25. DELIVERED UP BECAUSE OF OUR OFFENSES: The resurrection provided proof that God had accepted the sacrifice of His Son and would be able to be just and yet justify the ungodly.

UNLEASHING THE TEXT

1) What did God mean when He said to Abram, "I am your shield, your exceedingly great reward" (Genesis 15:1)? What was God promising to Abram by making this statement?

_____

_____

_____

_____

_____

2) If you had been Abram, knowing that you and your wife were both growing old, how would you have viewed God's promise that you would have a son?

_____

_____

_____

_____

_____

3) How would you have viewed God's promise concerning inheriting land? Would you have continued living as a nomad or done something different?

_____

_____

_____

_____

4) How does knowing the end of Abram's story change the way you view the doubts and fears that Abram faced? What should that teach us about the doubts and fears that we face?

_____

_____

_____

_____

EXPLORING THE MEANING

God's plans are bigger than we can understand. God revealed His plans to Abram concerning a son and a promised land, and these promises were immensely important to Abram. Yet they were actually a small part of God's larger plan, which was to bring a Redeemer to mankind to release us from sin and death.

Abram could not have understood this larger plan, yet his choice to obey or disobey would have profound ramifications. We saw this in study 1 when Abram jeopardized God's plan by giving his wife to another man. In this present study, we see how Abram's obedience furthered God's larger plan, eventually leading to our own salvation through Christ.

The principle here is that we must obey what God has called us to do, even though we may not see the bigger picture. God's plans extend beyond our own lives and beyond human history into eternity. Our part is simply to "trust and obey."

God works all things together for good to those who trust Him. This principle is closely related to the previous one, in that we are called to trust and obey. But the good news is that God's long-term plans for the human race do not override His short-term plans for us as individuals.

God's promises to Abram focused more on his descendants than on him personally—Abram himself never received any place that he could call home. However, at the same time, God gave Abram something far greater than any piece of real estate: He gave Abram a personal relationship with Himself.

The Lord does use His people to further His purposes in the lives of others, but He also pours out blessings on those people as He uses them. We will examine this in future studies as we see God draw Abram into an intimate relationship with Himself and use him in powerful ways in the land of Canaan. We will also see how the greatest blessing of all—an intimate communion with the Creator of all things—is still free to God's people today just as it was for Abram.

God's people are pilgrims and strangers on earth. God had promised that Abram's descendants would inherit the land of Canaan, yet Abram himself lived out his days in a tent, roaming from one place to another. Hebrews 11 tells us that he did this because his eyes were focused not on the land around him— even though it was going to become his—but on the eternal kingdom that God was preparing for His people.

This should be the attitude of God's people today as well. We must remember that this world is not our home; we are only here temporarily. The world is constantly pressuring us to put down roots and embrace the culture around us as though we were destined to dwell here forever. However, God's people must resist this attitude, because no man will remain on earth longer than the span of a human life.

When we accept Jesus as our Lord and Savior, we are born anew into the family of God and gain a new inheritance: God's Son Himself. We become heirs of the eternal kingdom of God, and nothing on this planet can compare with what awaits us. We must keep our eyes always focused on eternity and not allow the things of this world to interfere with our heavenly calling.

37

REFLECTING ON THE TEXT

5) What does it mean that God "accounted it to [Abram] for righteousness" (Genesis 15:6)? What insights does Paul add in Romans 4?

_____

_____

_____

_____

6) Notice that Abram "believed God" even before God sealed His covenant with the sacrificial ritual. Why did he believe God? On what did he base his faith?

_____

_____

_____

_____

7) Why did God call Abram to live in tents when He intended to give the land to his descendants anyway? Why did He not allow Abram to get settled into Canaan?

_____

_____

_____

_____

8) Why did God select Abram in the first place? Do you think it was something in Abram or something in God's gracious character that caused Him to bring the Messiah through Abram's family line?

_____

_____

_____

_____

PERSONAL RESPONSE

9) God performed the sacrificial ritual to permanently seal His covenant with Abram. What has He promised you? What has He done to seal those promises to you (beginning with the death of His Son on the cross)?

_____

_____

_____

_____

10) What things are most important to you in your life? In what ways are you living as a pilgrim on earth? In what ways are the things of this world distracting you?

_____

_____

_____

_____

4

HAGAR AND ISHMAEL
Genesis 16:1–16

DRAWING NEAR

When we feel that God is not moving according to our timetable, it can be tempting for us to try to jump in and "help" him bring things to pass. When have you done this in your life? What were the results?

_____

_____

_____

_____

THE CONTEXT

We have seen that God promised an heir to Abram many times over. The Lord had told Abraham that he would become a great nation and that his descendants would be so numerable that no man could hope to count them—like stars in the sky (see Genesis 15:4). God had also made it quite clear that this promise would come through a son of miraculous birth, a child born through the union of Abram and his wife, Sarai.

However, God had promised this many times over a period of at least ten years. Ten years is a long time to wait for a promised son to be born—especially when you are seventy-five years old to begin with! It would be a miracle if a woman in her late seventies gave birth to a child, especially if her husband were in his mid-eighties.

So it is not surprising to find that Sarai was beginning to have doubts about God's promise. To make matters worse, she and her husband began to *act* on their doubts, rather than on their faith. As a result, they found themselves taking matters into their own hands, falling into sin, and making bad decisions.

Sarai's scheme did lead to a birth, as her handmaid Hagar bore Abram a son named Ishmael. But God rejected Ishmael as the son of promise and made it clear that Ishmael could not share in Isaac's inheritance. As we will see in this study, Paul used these two young men to illustrate another truth of Scripture: man's works cannot play any part in God's plan of salvation, for we are saved by grace alone.

KEYS TO THE TEXT

Read Genesis 16:1–16, noting the key words and phrases indicated below.

> WRESTLING WITH DOUBT: *Abram and Sarai are still waiting for the appearance of Isaac. It's been at least ten years since God promised a son, so they decide that they should help God along.*

16:1. NOW SARAI, ABRAM'S WIFE: It is important to note that the events in this passage take place before Abram's circumcision and change of name in Genesis 17, which we will discuss in the next study. This is an important distinction to understand, because the circumcision marked a new relationship between God and Abram—a sort of "rebirth" in which Abram received his new name. This distinction will become more important as we move into our New Testament passages.

HAD BORNE HIM NO CHILDREN: God had promised Abram that he would have a son and countless descendants, but that son would not arrive until after Abram had been circumcised, cutting off the flesh. This was part of God's picture of the final redemption plan, when we are reborn into the family of Christ.

AN EGYPTIAN MAIDSERVANT: The nation of Egypt is frequently used in Scripture to represent the world's system. There is a good possibility that Hagar was one of the servants that Pharaoh gave to Abram during his sojourn there when Abram was trying to escape a famine in Canaan.

2. THE LORD HAS RESTRAINED ME FROM BEARING CHILDREN: This statement from Sarai was technically true, for the Lord is the giver of life. Yet it reflected a lack of faith in her thinking—she was growing impatient waiting for the Lord to fulfill His promise. There may even be a degree of resentment in her words, as though she was blaming God for her childlessness.

I SHALL OBTAIN: Sarai's focus was more on herself and her plans than on the larger picture. God had promised more than a son for Abram and Sarai: He had promised an entire nation and descendants that could not be numbered. In the bigger picture still, He had promised a Redeemer—the Seed who would one day save mankind from sin. God's plan certainly included the personal longings of Abram and Sarai for a son, yet it was far, far bigger than that. The results of Sarai's scheme would also last far longer than she anticipated.

CHILDREN BY HER: God had told Abram, "One who will come from your own body shall be your heir" (Genesis 15:4). Technically, the son born through Hagar would be from Abram's own body, but the Lord meant that the heir would be born through his proper union with his own wife, Sarai. The Lord had decreed in the garden of Eden that a man would "be joined to his wife, and they shall become one flesh" (Genesis 2:24), and Abram would have understood this from the Lord's promise.

SARAI TAKES CHARGE: Sarai now puts into action her plan of assisting God in the business of producing an heir.

ABRAM HEEDED THE VOICE OF SARAI: Abram repeated the sin of Adam by placing himself under the spiritual authority of his wife (see Genesis 3:17). The Lord had just come to Abram in a vision and made a formal covenant with him (see Genesis 15). God had bolstered Abram's faith and encouraged him, but then Abram turned right around and allowed his wife to take the lead.

3. SARAI, ABRAM'S WIFE, TOOK HAGAR HER MAID: Eve had perceived a problem that didn't exist, thanks to the direct lies of the serpent, and she took matters into her own hands to resolve that nonexistent problem. Likewise, Sarai perceived there was a problem with God's promise being fulfilled, so she took matters into her own hands to resolve it. The results in both cases were disastrous

and affected all of mankind. As we will see, the son born through Hagar will lead to the Arabic nations, which are still at war with Israel even today.

4. HER MISTRESS BECAME DESPISED: This was just the beginning of woes from this bad plan.

5. MY WRONG BE UPON YOU: This statement from Sarai was, of course, grossly unfair, as the entire plan was hers in the first place. Yet it is also quite literally true, for the Lord would hold Abram responsible for abdicating his spiritual authority in the home, just as He held Adam responsible in Eden.

GOD MEETS HAGAR: *Hagar flees from Sarai's harsh treatment and goes into the wilderness. There she meets the Angel of the Lord.*

7. THE ANGEL OF THE LORD: This special individual spoke as though He were distinct from Yahweh, yet also spoke in the first person as though He were indeed to be identified as Yahweh Himself. Hagar, in seeing this angel, believed she had seen God. The Angel of the Lord, who does not appear after the birth of Christ, is often identified as the preincarnate Christ.

SHUR: This location was south of Palestine and east of Egypt, which meant that Hagar attempted to return home to Egypt.

9. HAGAR, SARAI'S MAID ... RETURN TO YOUR MISTRESS, AND SUBMIT: The Angel's salutation and instruction indicated that He considered the mistress-servant relationship between Sarai and Hagar to be intact. Rebelling and absconding was not the solution.

GOD'S PLAN FOR HAGAR: *The Angel of the Lord now reveals the plan that God has for Hagar and her descendants.*

10. I WILL MULTIPLY: Hagar might have been a servant, but she would also become the mother of many, thus making Abram the father of two groups of innumerable descendants.

11. CALL HIS NAME ISHMAEL: This name meant "God hears." Hagar, the servant, would never forget how God had heard her cry of affliction.

12. A WILD MAN ... AGAINST EVERY MAN: Ishmael would be like the untamable desert onager (wild donkey), with a fiercely aggressive and independent nature. Ishmael's Arabic descendants would also exhibit these traits.

13. YOU-ARE-THE-GOD-WHO-SEES: Hagar recognized the Angel as none other than God Himself, and her astonishment at having been the object of His gracious attention led her to ascribe this name to Him. The revelation also led her to call Him "The One Who Lives and Sees Me."

15. HIS SON ... ISHMAEL: Ishmael was born c. 2079 BC.

16. EIGHTY-SIX YEARS OLD: Abram was seventy-five years old when he left Haran (see Genesis 12:4).

GOING DEEPER

Read Galatians 3:29–4:5, 21–31, noting the key words and phrases indicated below.

ABRAHAM'S HEIRS: Christians are adopted into the family of God and inherit all the blessings that He gave to Abraham.

3:29. YOU ARE ABRAHAM'S SEED: Paul writes that when we accept Jesus as our Lord and Savior, we become adopted into the family of God. We are spiritual descendants of Abraham in the sense that we follow the pattern of his faith and are heirs to all the promises of God.

4:1. THE HEIR: Paul used Isaac and Ishmael in a symbolic way to represent grace and legalism, respectively.

4. BORN UNDER THE LAW: Paul was referring to the law of Moses, which God gave to the Israelites during their exodus from Egypt. The Old Testament law consisted of many animal sacrifices and other stipulations that God required of His people if they were to remain in fellowship with Him. Jesus was literally "born under the law" in the sense that the law of Moses was still in effect when He was born. However, after His death and resurrection, that law was abolished.

ISAAC AND ISHMAEL AS SYMBOLS: Paul uses Ishmael and Isaac to illustrate the fact that Christians are under grace and set free from the law of Moses.

4:22. TWO SONS: Ishmael and Isaac, respectively.

23. BORN ACCORDING TO THE FLESH: As we have seen, Ishmael was born because Sarai and Abram tried to take God's will into their own hands.

45

He thus represents legalism in Paul's letter, because legalism is man's attempt to earn righteousness apart from God's grace.

24. SYMBOLIC: That is, Paul was using Isaac and Ishmael as symbolic examples of doctrine. He was not suggesting that they were not literal or historical people.

THE TWO COVENANTS: The first covenant was the law of Moses, given at Mount Sinai during Israel's exodus from Egypt. The second covenant was one of grace, given on Mount Calvary when Christ died for our sins.

GIVES BIRTH TO BONDAGE: The law of Moses brought bondage to the people of Israel in the sense that they had an endless array of works to perform in order to obtain forgiveness for sins. Good works are the natural outgrowth of saving faith (see James 2:17–23), but they are utterly powerless to save us from sin. We are saved by grace alone.

25. HAGAR IS MOUNT SINAI: Again, Hagar symbolically represents the law of Moses, which was given to Israel on Mount Sinai.

GRACE AND LEGALISM: Paul continues his illustration to show how legalism only leads the Christian into slavery and bondage.

IS IN BONDAGE WITH HER CHILDREN: It is significant that God would later tell Abram to send away Hagar and Ishmael (see Genesis 21). Hagar was a bondwoman, an indentured servant, and did not have the inherent rights that Sarai had. Hagar's son also was a bondservant, with no inherent rights of a natural son. God told Abraham to send them away because He would not allow anyone but Isaac to enjoy Abraham's inheritance. Paul applied this teaching to the conflict between grace and legalism, showing that mankind's good works do not and cannot play a part—not even the smallest part—in our salvation. "For by grace you have been saved through faith, and that not of yourselves; it is the gift of God, not of works, lest anyone should boast" (Ephesians 2:8–9).

26. THE JERUSALEM ABOVE: Paul was referring to the eternal kingdom of God. "By faith Abraham obeyed when he was called to go out to the place which he would receive as an inheritance. And he went out, not knowing where he was going. By faith he dwelt in the land of promise as in a foreign country, dwelling in tents with Isaac and Jacob, the heirs with him of the same promise;

for he waited for the city which has foundations, whose builder and maker is God" (Hebrews 11:8–10).

29. PERSECUTED HIM: The flesh and spirit are always at war within a Christian, just as Ishmael persecuted Isaac. Similarly, the law of Moses cannot work together with the grace of God to bring about our salvation. Legalism only takes Christians back into bondage and is constantly at war with the Spirit.

UNLEASHING THE TEXT

1) If you had been in Sarai's place, how would you have felt about God's promises for a son? Would you have tried to give God some help?

_____

_____

_____

_____

_____

_____

2) How did Sarai's solution to the problem of her childlessness show lack of faith in her thinking? How did it reveal her shortsightedness in God's larger plans?

_____

_____

_____

_____

_____

_____

3) What was the problem with Abram allowing Sarai to take the lead in this matter? How did he repeat the error of Adam in the garden of Eden?

_____

_____

_____

_____

4) What promise did God make to Hagar in the wilderness? Why did He command her to return to Sarai?

_____

_____

_____

_____

EXPLORING THE MEANING

It is not a sin to have questions about what God is doing, but acting out of doubt will lead to sin. As we have seen throughout the story of Abram, God sometimes asks us to trust Him to accomplish the impossible. We are only made of dust, and it is natural for us to have doubts at times as to how God will fulfill His promises.

The problem is not in having occasional doubts or questions, but in *acting* on those doubts or questions out of fear or frustration. Sarai and Abram had the choice between acting on their doubts and acting on their faith. Acting on faith would have meant doing essentially nothing apart from maintaining normal marital relations. The difficult aspect of that, however, is the very fact of *doing nothing*. There are times when the most difficult course of action is *no* action at all—to wait patiently on God's timing.

Yet that is precisely the course that Abram and Sarai should have followed, patiently continuing to wait for God's own timetable. Instead, they focused on their doubts, persuaded themselves that God's promise could not be fulfilled without their help, and took matters into their own hands. As we have seen, that particular sin had consequences that will exist until the end of time.

We can never predict the consequences of sin. Sarai probably did not think that her plan concerning Hagar was sinful, and she certainly never thought that it would bring about suffering for her own family. Abram may well have understood that Sarai's plan was sinful, yet he did not stop to count the cost of disobedience.

There are times when we persuade ourselves that "this one little bit" of sinful behavior won't hurt "just this once." However, Abram's single act of disobedience with Hagar led to countless deaths and acts of persecution that have continued for several thousand years to this present day. Again, consider what a small sin Adam committed when he merely ate a piece of fruit.

Humans are specialists at self-deception and self-justification. We can always excuse and condone the "little sins" that we commit. However, we should keep in mind that we cannot predict what consequences each "one little sin" may produce—such as how many innocent people may suffer, or how long the ripples may continue, or even what price we may pay ourselves.

Christians are called to do good works, but our good works can never save us. As Paul tells us in Galatians 4, we are saved by faith—and faith alone—through the grace of God. By "saved," we mean that our sins have been permanently forgiven, once and for all. We have been brought into an eternal relationship with God because Jesus paid the price for our sins on the cross.

This salvation could not have been accomplished by any human being who has ever walked this planet—with one exception. This is because every human who has ever lived has been a sinner, and a sinner cannot pay for someone else's sins, nor can he pay for his own. The only Person who could accomplish this was the one Person who lived a sinless life: Jesus.

God is faithful to apply Jesus' payment to our sin-debt when we repent of our sins and ask Him for forgiveness. This step of repentance is accomplished by faith alone. There is nothing whatsoever that any person can ever do to accomplish it except to receive it in faith.

REFLECTING ON THE TEXT

5) What sorts of "help" might have been legitimate for Abram and Sarai to give in fulfilling God's promises? What made Sarai's plan not legitimate?

_____

_____

_____

_____

_____

6) Why do you think Abram consented to Sarai's plan if he understood it was wrong? How might he have justified it in his own mind?

_____

_____

_____

_____

_____

7) In view of Paul's discussion of grace versus the law, why was it important for Hagar and Ishmael (who are symbolic of the law) to later be sent away from Isaac (who is symbolic of grace)?

_____

_____

_____

8. Why did Paul use Isaac and Ishmael as symbols of grace and legalism, respectively? How does this symbolism help you understand these concepts?

_____

_____

_____

_____

PERSONAL RESPONSE

9) With what doubts are you struggling? What course of action does the Lord want you to take?

_____

_____

_____

_____

10) Do you understand the distinction between *good works* (loving, grace-filled obedience) and *legalism*? Which of these does your life reflect?

_____

_____

_____

_____

5

COVENANT AND OBEDIENCE
Genesis 17:1–18:15

DRAWING NEAR

In today's reading, God gives Abram and Sarai new names. What are nicknames that you have been given in the past? How did you feel about being called those names?

_____

_____

_____

_____

THE CONTEXT

Previously, we witnessed the Lord making a covenant with Abram concerning his descendants and their future in the land of Canaan. That covenant was unconditional, for God alone promised it to Abram and sealed it with a ritual involving animal sacrifice. Abram didn't need to do anything in the process except be a witness.

Now, God comes to Abram to reiterate that covenant. However, this time God emphasizes Abram's need to keep the covenant and reveals what the sign of that covenant will be—namely, circumcision. The rite of circumcision (which involved the removal of the male foreskin) set the Jewish people apart as those specially chosen by God. It also symbolized the need to cut away sin and be cleansed. God commanded Abram and his descendants to keep the covenant that He had made with them.

Sadly, there were many times throughout Israel's history that the nation was unfaithful to this covenant and the other covenants that God had made with them. Nonetheless, God's faithfulness to the Abrahamic Covenant never wavered.

The passage we will read today again underscores the intimate fellowship that Abram enjoyed with God. We saw this previously when God appeared to Abram in visions, but this time He actually speaks with Abram face to face. In addition, God gives him something else: a new name. God changes his name from "Abram" to "Abraham," and his wife goes from "Sarai" to "Sarah." These new names symbolize the fact that God has a special purpose for them as the parents of His chosen nation.

In this study, we will look at the historical event of God's covenant with Abraham and then move into the New Testament to find out what it means to us today.

Keys to the Text

Read Genesis 17:1–18:15, noting the key words and phrases indicated below.

> God Speaks to Abram: *Once again, God appears to Abram. By this time Abram is ninety-nine and Sarai is eighty-nine.*

17:1. Abram was ninety-nine years old: Thirteen years have passed since the episode with Hagar and Ishmael.

The Lord appeared to Abram: We are not told in this case just *how* God appeared to Abram, but it was most likely in the form of a dream or a vision. We do know that God appeared previously in dreams and visions (see Genesis 15:1, 12). It is likely that God had *not* appeared in physical form to Abram up to this time.

WALK BEFORE ME: The Hebrew word translated "before Me" means "face." God was saying, "Walk in My face—keep My face before you at all times, and remember that My face is always looking toward you."

BE BLAMELESS: This word means "complete, whole, having integrity." God did not expect Abraham to live a sin-free life from that point on but that his life would be characterized by patterns of righteousness. Similarly, God does not expect Christians to never fall into sin after salvation. He does, however, command us to order our entire lives around His Word. Moreover, we have been covered in the righteousness of Christ, and our sins have been cleansed because of His death on our behalf.

NEW NAMES: God signifies His special purposes for Abram—as the father of His chosen people—by giving him and Sarai new names.

2. I WILL MAKE MY COVENANT BETWEEN ME AND YOU: In Genesis 15, God performed a ritual for Abram that sealed His unwavering commitment to fulfill the promises He had made. The Lord now reiterated the elements of that covenant: Abram would have many descendants, those descendants would inherit Canaan, and they would be a blessing to the nations. This reaffirmation of God's divine promises brackets the change of name that will happen next.

5. YOUR NAME SHALL BE ABRAHAM: Abram means "high father," while Abraham means "father of many nations." It is significant that God gave Abram a new name because it underscored the fact that God had a special purpose for him as the father of His chosen people. In ancient times, a ruler might assign a subject a new name to indicate that the subject was now his property. The same was true of Abram, who was God's chosen servant. God would use him to bring great blessing to the world.

NEW INSTRUCTIONS: The Lord adds important details to covenant with Abraham—details that will instruct him and his descendants as to how they are to respond to God's promises.

7. I WILL ESTABLISH MY COVENANT: It was God who had initiated the unique relationship between Himself and Abraham. He was the one who chose Abraham, not the other way around.

AN EVERLASTING COVENANT: God states that His special relationship with Abraham's descendants will last as long as the earth itself and even into eternity. This promise will be realized in its fullness during the future Millennial Kingdom, when Jesus Christ reigns on the earth for a thousand years. At that time, all of Israel will be saved (see Romans 11:26).

8. ALL THE LAND OF CANAAN: God's reaffirmation of His covenant promises to Abraham did not occur without mention of the land being deeded by divine right to him and his descendants as an everlasting possession.

9. YOU SHALL KEEP MY COVENANT: Despite repeated disobedience by the patriarchs and the nation, God's faithfulness to His covenant commitment never wavered. Although the nation of Israel would be characterized by times of disobedience, God was true to His Word. There was always an obedient remnant of faithful Israelites who walked in the example of their father, Abraham.

CIRCUMCISION: In reiterating His covenant with Abraham, God will now institute the sign of that covenant: circumcision.

10. THIS IS MY COVENANT WHICH YOU SHALL KEEP: Here the Lord begins to define the new covenant.

CIRCUMCISED: As previously stated, circumcision is the removal of the male foreskin. This practice was not entirely new during this period of history, but the special religious and theocratic significance that God applied to it was entirely new. In this way, the Lord identified the circumcised as belonging to the physical and ethnical lineage of Abraham.

11. IT SHALL BE A SIGN OF THE COVENANT: There was nothing magical about this operation—being circumcised did not bring about some mystical transformation in the male or purchase a relationship with God. It was done solely as an outward sign of the covenant, just as a wedding ring is the outward sign of a marriage covenant.

12. EIGHT DAYS OLD: From a medical perspective this is the ideal time to perform this operation, as it heals quickly and produces the least pain possible. However, it also suggests that it is good for a person to commit himself to the Lord at an early age. "It is good for a man to bear the yoke in his youth" (Lamentations 3:27).

EVERY MALE CHILD IN YOUR GENERATIONS: Here we see again the importance of parental teaching concerning the ways of the Lord. Circumcision represents a decision that each man must make for himself—whether or not to serve the Lord faithfully—yet it is also a decision that is made by the parents for the child. Parents bear a significant share of the responsibility for the spiritual decisions their children will make.

13. MUST BE CIRCUMCISED: The Lord now underscored this principle even further, making it clear that His people are accountable to ensure that their entire household is brought under the teaching of God's Word. Parents bear a significant share of the responsibility for helping their children make wise spiritual decisions.

14. THAT PERSON SHALL BE CUT OFF: A person's relationship with God is serious business. The Lord was making it clear that any Israelite who was not willing to obey Him in this important way evidenced the fact that he was not a true follower of God, and thus was to be distanced from those who willingly submitted to God's commands. To be cut off meant to be disinherited, disowned, and removed from the presence of God and His people.

HE HAS BROKEN MY COVENANT: This did not mean that Abraham's descendants would not inherit the land. Rather, it meant that any of Abraham's descendants who were uncircumcised would not inherit a relationship with God.

15. SARAH SHALL BE HER NAME: Sarai can mean "my princess," whereas Sarah means "princess." This is a subtle distinction, perhaps indicating that as the mother of many nations, she would become a princess to more than just her husband. The bigger issue, however, is that the Lord was changing her name as well as her husband's, indicating that she, too, was chosen by God for a special purpose.

GOD'S WAY OR NO WAY: *The Lord once again makes it apparent that He has one chosen seed—and only one—through whom the promise will be fulfilled.*

18. OH, THAT ISHMAEL MIGHT LIVE BEFORE YOU: Abraham was still struggling to comprehend how God was going to give him a son through Sarah at their advanced ages. His doubting mind resorted to an easy solution: Ishmael, who had already been born. But God is not hindered by simple impossibilities,

and He had a good reason for rejecting Ishmael or any other person except the one of His choosing.

19. NO, SARAH YOUR WIFE SHALL BEAR YOU A SON: Again, patiently but firmly rejecting Abraham's alternative solution, God emphatically settled the matter by bracketing His gracious bestowal of much posterity to Ishmael with affirmations that, indeed, Sarah's son would be the heir of the everlasting covenant.

CALL HIS NAME ISAAC: For the first time, God named the promised son. Isaac means "he laughs," an appropriate reminder to Abraham of his initial faithless reaction to God's promise.

I WILL ESTABLISH MY COVENANT WITH HIM: Once again we are confronted with the fact that God was sovereignly at work in determining through whom He would bring about His chosen seed. Abraham had other sons, just as Isaac would have two sons, but the covenant would extend only to the one chosen from each generation. This foreshadowed the fact that there is ultimately only one way to find peace with God, and that is through His only begotten Son—the final Chosen Seed of Israel's race.

23. THAT VERY SAME DAY: Without delay, Abraham fully carried out God's command on himself and on all the men of his house.

GUESS WHO'S COMING TO DINNER: Some time later, God, accompanied by two angels, comes to Abraham and has dinner with him.

18:1. THE LORD APPEARED TO HIM: Abraham was seated outside his tent when three men appeared. One of those men was God Himself, appearing in human form. Abraham invited the men to dine with him.

TREES OF MAMRE: A distinctively large grove of trees owned by Mamre the Amorite, located approximately nineteen miles southwest of Jerusalem at Hebron.

3. MY LORD: Although perhaps first used as the customary respectful address of a host to a visitor, later in their interchange it was used knowingly by Abraham of his true and sovereign Lord.

10. ACCORDING TO THE TIME OF LIFE: The Lord promised that Abraham and Sarah would give birth to their promised son within the year—and He kept His promise.

SARAH HAD PASSED THE AGE OF CHILDBEARING: This had precisely been the Lord's intention in His promises to Abraham concerning an heir. He allowed the couple to get well beyond the point where it was physically possible for them to bear children because He wanted the birth of Isaac to be an undeniable miracle. This would be a foreshadowing of the miraculous virgin birth of Jesus Himself. The Lord also wanted to stretch the faith of both Abraham and Sarah in this process, teaching them "with God all things are possible" (Mark 10:27).

HE KNOWS OUR THOUGHTS: Sarah, sitting inside the tent, laughs silently when she hears the Lord's promise. Yet the Lord knows her thoughts.

12. SARAH LAUGHED: We can hardly blame Sarah for this laughter. If someone told a ninety-year-old woman today that she was going to have a baby within a year, laughter might be among the most gentle of responses that one could expect. Abraham himself had laughed not long before when the Lord appeared to him (see Genesis 17:17).

WITHIN HERSELF: That is, she did not laugh aloud.

13. WHY DID SARAH LAUGH: The Lord knows even our most intimate thoughts (see Psalm 94:11). In this instance, He went beyond Sarah's laughter and quoted the very thoughts of her mind. This must have been disconcerting for her as she sat inside the tent, out of view of the strange men who were outside.

14. IS ANYTHING TOO HARD FOR THE LORD: This is at the core of this difficult lesson for Sarah and Abraham, and the Lord insisted they both learn the lesson fully. It is an important lesson for all God's children, but it was also important in the prophecies concerning the Messiah, whose birth would be the most miraculous, impossible human birth of all time. Compared with Jesus' virgin birth, Isaac's birth was a piece of cake.

15. I DID NOT LAUGH: It is understandable that Sarah was frightened at this point. This Man who was speaking to her husband was clearly more than a mere mortal. Yet she was still not justified in lying—even though it was technically only a "half lie." Sarah had laughed *inwardly,* not literally out loud. But God does not countenance lies in any form, not even when they are half true. This was the same problem that Abraham had—more than once—in telling people that Sarah was his sister but not his wife.

GOING DEEPER

Read Colossians 2:9–14, noting the key words and phrases indicated below.

THE DEITY OF CHRIST: In this passage, Paul addresses the issue of circumcision and how it applies to Christians today.

2:9. ALL THE FULLNESS OF THE GODHEAD BODILY: Jesus is God, part of the Trinity of the Godhead. Many cults claim that Jesus was the *Son* of God without actually being part of the Godhead, but this denies a fundamental doctrine of the Christian church. If Jesus is not God, then He cannot forgive sin, because all sin is against God (see Psalm 51:4). If Jesus is not God, then all that Paul was saying in this chapter is null and void.

10. YOU ARE COMPLETE IN HIM: This ties back to God's covenant with Abraham, where the Lord said, "I am Almighty God; walk before Me and be blameless [made complete]" (Genesis 17:1). Through the sacrificial death of Jesus, we are now blameless and complete in the eyes of the Father—our entire debt has been paid, and we are washed as clean as if we had never sinned.

SPIRITUAL CIRCUMCISION: Abraham's circumcision was merely a physical picture of a deeper spiritual truth. Paul now tells us what it symbolized.

THE CIRCUMCISION MADE WITHOUT HANDS: The circumcision of the Old Testament law was merely a physical picture of an eternal and spiritual truth. Circumcision symbolized man's need for cleansing of the heart and was the outward sign of that cleansing of sin that comes by faith in God. In Christ, this eternal truth is fulfilled—made complete—in each person who accepts Him as Savior. At salvation, believers undergo a spiritual circumcision by "putting off the body of the sins of the flesh." This is the new birth and the new creation in conversion.

PUTTING OFF THE BODY THE SINS OF THE FLESH: Circumcision involved cutting off the male foreskin, which was representative of the fact that the sinful nature (which is transmitted through the seed of the man) must be cut off. By removing this piece of flesh, Old Testament Jews were symbolizing the fact that God required His people to completely remove the sinful nature. Of course, a person cannot actually physically cut off his human nature, as we are born into the flesh of Adam. Thus, physical circumcision could not eternally save anyone—it was merely a picture of spiritual truth.

THE CIRCUMCISION OF CHRIST: Circumcision could not change a person's sinful nature, but God can! Only God can offer a person a *new* birth into the *new* Adam (being Christ)—a new life that is devoid of Adam's sinful nature. This is the "circumcision of Christ," which provides a new birth for anyone who accepts Him as Lord and Savior.

12. RAISED WITH HIM THROUGH FAITH: Once the Adamic nature has been put to death, we are raised into a new birth. For Christians this is symbolized in baptism, when we come out of the water as Christ burst out of the tomb.

13. HAVING FORGIVEN YOU ALL TRESPASSES: Again, only God can forgive sin, so Jesus has to be God if the New Testament is to be proved true. This teaching is the very reason the Jews wanted to crucify Christ: "The scribes and the Pharisees began to reason, saying, 'Who is this who speaks blasphemies? Who can forgive sins but God alone?'" (Luke 5:21). "Therefore the Jews sought all the more to kill Him, because He not only broke the Sabbath, but also said that God was His Father, making Himself equal with God" (John 5:18).

UNLEASHING THE TEXT

1) Why did God reiterate His covenant with Abram? What additional information did He provide to Abram on this occasion?

_____

_____

_____

_____

_____

2) Why did God rename Abram and Sarai? What does this symbolize?

_____

_____

_____

_____

3) What did physical circumcision symbolize for the Old Testament Jew? What spiritual reality did circumcision represent?

_____

_____

_____

_____

_____

4) How would you have reacted if a stranger arrived for dinner and began to tell you what you were thinking? What does this reveal about God's feelings toward Sarah?

_____

_____

_____

_____

_____

EXPLORING THE MEANING

The flesh cannot inherit the kingdom of God. When the Bible speaks about the flesh, it is referring to our sinful nature. We have inherited our human flesh from Adam, the father of the human race. Unfortunately, we inherited more than just Adam's physical flesh—we also inherited his decision to commit sin. Genesis makes it clear that like brings forth like, meaning that one type of creature can only reproduce its own kind.

This means that Adam and his descendants can only give birth to sinners because they are sinners themselves. God cannot tolerate the presence of sin in any degree whatsoever, which is a terrible situation for us as Adam's descendants to be in, because we are born in sin and cannot escape our human heritage. Therefore, we are eternally cut off from the presence of God.

There is only one hope for mankind: we must find some way of removing our sinful nature—our flesh—if we are to enter God's presence. This is precisely what the Lord was symbolizing when He commanded Abraham to be circumcised. The fulfillment of this symbol came several thousand years later through Jesus Christ.

Christians are born again into the Second Adam. This leads us into the next principle, which is that Jesus made possible what for man was impossible: a change in our nature. This is something that is utterly impossible under the laws of creation. "A leopard cannot change its spots," as the old saying goes, and neither can a man change the fact that he is born in the image of Adam.

God makes this miracle possible by offering us the opportunity to be *born again* into a new image—born a second time to the Second Adam, God's Son, Jesus Christ (see 1 Corinthians 15:45). In order to be born again, however, our old self must first die. These truths are symbolized in baptism. To symbolize dying to our flesh, we go down into the water (as Christ went into the tomb in death) as the old man, the old Adam. To symbolize our rebirth through the power of the Spirit, we come up out of the water (as Christ burst out of the tomb) into the person of the new man, the family of the Last Adam, being reborn through the power of the Spirit.

When we accept Christ as Savior, we put to death our sinful nature and are born again into a new nature, the image of Christ. Just as we could not remove our original natures by our own efforts, so also we can never lose our new nature—we are reborn forever into the image of God's Son, Jesus Christ.

Jesus is God. This truth is absolute bedrock to the Christian faith. Only God can forgive sins, so the One who offers forgiveness of sins must be God if that offer is to be real. Only God can "change the leopard's spots," removing our Adamic nature and giving us a new Godnature.

Groups who teach that Jesus is not God—such as the Mormons and Jehovah's Witnesses—are preaching a false gospel. The New Testament is clear on the deity of Christ, as Paul demonstrated in the passages we examined during this study (see Colossians 2:9). Jesus Himself forgave the sins of His followers (see Luke 5:21), and He accepted the worship of men who proclaimed Him God (see John 20:28).

It is vital that Christians understand and cling to this important fact, for it is at the very basis of our faith. When we proclaim Jesus as Lord, we are proclaiming Him as Creator God.

REFLECTING ON THE TEXT

5) What does it mean to be "born again"? What is involved in becoming born again?

_____

_____

_____

_____

6) How do we know that Jesus is God? Give scriptural support.

_____

_____

_____

_____

7) Why did God not command Sarah to do something in His reiteration of the covenant? What does this teach us about spiritual headship?

_____

_____

_____

_____

8) Considering that God's promise involved giving birth to a son, why is it significant that Abraham had to be circumcised before that promise was fulfilled?

_____

_____

_____

_____

PERSONAL RESPONSE

9) Have you been born again? If not, why? What have you got to lose? What have you got to gain?

_____

_____

_____

_____

10) If you are a Christian, have you been baptized? If not, why? What is holding you back from obeying this command of Scripture and publicly symbolizing your union with Christ?

_____

_____

_____

_____

6

THE FAITH OF ABRAHAM
Genesis 18:16–33

DRAWING NEAR

Intercession is the act of intervening on behalf of someone. When is a time you have interceded for another person? What were the results?

_____

_____

_____

_____

THE CONTEXT

We have been studying a number of events in Abraham's life to get a bigger picture of the history surrounding God's chosen people—leading to those of us who are adopted into the spiritual family of Abraham through the rebirth offered by Jesus. Now we will take a look at an episode that reveals a bit more about the man himself.

Abraham was called "the friend of God" (James 2:23), and God chose him to be the founding father of His chosen people. This naturally raises the question, why Abraham? What was so special about him that set him apart from the world around him? What did he do to deserve such honor? The primary answer, of course, is *nothing*!

Abraham did not deserve honor from God any more than we do. God chose him because of His grace, not through Abraham's own merit. Yet God *grew* Abraham into a person of merit—a man whose life is an example to us today. Thus, it is worthwhile to ask ourselves what it means to be a friend of God.

Abraham was, first and foremost, a man of faith. We have seen that in several of our previous studies as we witnessed Abraham believing God's promise for a son even when it seemed impossible. Abraham was also a man of obedience and quick to do what the Lord commanded. Fortunately for us, he was also a man of flesh—a man who sometimes *didn't* obey completely what the Lord told him to do. In this we can find encouragement and realize that God chooses ordinary people to be His friends, even when we fall short from time to time.

In this study, we will discover another aspect of Abraham's life: he interceded for others. When God visited him on His way with two angels to pour down judgment on Sodom and Gomorrah, Abraham could easily have minded his own business, "stayed out of it," and allowed God to do what He thought best. Abraham could have gone the other direction and felt proud that he was so much more righteous than those Sodomites. But instead, he humbly approached the Lord and began to plead for Him to withhold His righteous judgment from the cities of Sodom and Gomorrah.

Abraham's faith led to God's declaration that he was righteous, but that faith quite naturally worked itself out in deeds—and the two together encompass the righteousness of Abraham. The friend of God, as we will see, is one who has both faith *and* works, since genuine faith results in heartfelt obedience.

KEYS TO THE TEXT

Read Genesis 18:16–33, noting the key words and phrases indicated below.

> *SHALL I TELL HIM: Here we are given a privileged glimpse into God's mind as He sought to determine whether or not to reveal His plans—and His character—to His friend Abraham.*

18:16. ROSE FROM THERE AND LOOKED TOWARD SODOM: Abraham was living in Mamre at this point (see the map in the Introduction). The exact locations of Sodom and Gomorrah are not known, but they were probably situated at the southern tip of what is now the Dead Sea (or Salt Sea). Mamre was located in the high hills above the Jordan Valley, and Sodom was perhaps twenty-five to thirty-five miles away.

17. SHALL I HIDE FROM ABRAHAM: The question God asked was probably rhetorical, meaning, "Now that I have brought Abraham into my confidence, I cannot exclude him from this event." The Lord's reason for permitting Abraham to know of judgment in advance underscored his special role in the plan of God.

18. ALL THE NATIONS OF THE EARTH SHALL BE BLESSED IN HIM: God was about to reveal to Abraham another aspect of His character: justice. In addition to this, as we shall see, Abraham was about to learn what *his* role would be in becoming a blessing to the nations. An important part of that blessing would be a clearer understanding of the character of God Himself. Prior to Abraham, God's direct interactions with men had been limited, but He was now planning to reveal more of Himself to Abraham and his descendants. Their role would be to tell the world what He revealed.

19. I HAVE KNOWN HIM: The word "know" here implies a deep and intimate relationship. It is also used in Scripture to describe a husband's intimacy with his wife. God's relationship with Abraham was deeply intimate. He understood Abraham better than Abraham understood himself.

IN ORDER THAT HE MAY COMMAND HIS CHILDREN: God here revealed the very reason why He had selected Abraham: so that Abraham would "command" his entire household in the way of the Lord. It is significant that the Lord did not expect Abraham to *ask* or to *suggest* how his household should live. Rather, he was to *command* them, which again implies that the head of the household should have strong spiritual authority. This goes against modern notions of marriage and childrearing, which teach us that children should be offered various options but allowed to choose their own "path." That is not the sort of leadership God expected of Abraham.

KEEP THE WAY OF THE LORD: God wanted Abraham to ensure that his household *kept* the way of the Lord, which implies that they might otherwise lose the way. This has happened in Western society, as an entire generation is growing up without any knowledge of God's Word and God's ways. The Hebrew word translated "keep" here literally means "to hedge about with thorns."

In other words, God is warning us that we must deliberately guard and protect the way of the Lord within our homes, lest our children and grandchildren lose the way.

TO DO RIGHTEOUSNESS AND JUSTICE: God was about to demonstrate both of these aspects of His character. He wanted His children to live righteously, which was *not* what the Sodomites were doing. Their wickedness was about to bring the justice of God down on their own heads. It is important to recognize that God expects His people to exhibit both aspects of His character as well—righteousness *and* justice.

> GOD'S PLAN: *The Lord explains to Abraham why He has come— He is going to visit Sodom and Gomorrah to see whether they are as wicked as reported.*

20. THE OUTCRY AGAINST SODOM AND GOMORRAH IS GREAT: The iniquity of the two cities had reached the point of no return before the Lord. Men tend to grow wickeder as they persuade themselves that there is no God in heaven to hold them accountable. (This is one of the reasons why Satan has worked so hard to deceive modern mankind with the false belief of evolution.) However, God let Abraham know that He was always aware of people's actions—good or bad—and that persistent wickedness raises an actual outcry before His throne in heaven.

21. I WILL GO DOWN NOW AND SEE: God went a step further than merely listening to the outcry against Sodom—He came in physical form to meet with Abraham and enact judgment on Sodom. Typically, when God came to earth in the flesh, it was for the purpose of judgment. He came to the garden of Eden to confront Adam for committing the first sin (see Genesis 3). Later, He would go to Babel to investigate the great tower that men were building out of their colossal pride (see Genesis 11). Ultimately, He would come to earth as a baby for the most costly act of judgment, and God's justice would fall fully on the shoulders of His Son. In every case, however, God's visit was an act of grace and mercy, as He always went beyond what was required.

22. THE MEN TURNED AWAY: This refers to the two angels who were with the Lord.

ABRAHAM DRAWS NEAR: God had treated Abraham with intimate friendship, and here Abraham responds. His first step is to take another step—nearer to God.

ABRAHAM STILL STOOD BEFORE THE LORD: Abraham had an intimate friendship with God that not even the angels shared. He stood almost as an equal before his Creator, speaking to Him face-to-face as one man speaks to another. Abraham had become God's personal friend.

23. ABRAHAM CAME NEAR: Abraham would now take that intimacy one step farther and deliberately draw himself closer to God. The Hebrew implies the deepest form of adoration and worship. This was the very reason why God chose Abraham to be His special envoy in the world—He wanted His children to deliberately draw closer to Him in worship and admiration.

WOULD YOU: Abraham began a conversation with the Lord in which he interceded for Sodom, yet he was also trying to get to know God better. He was, in effect, asking God about His character and trying to understand the balance between justice and mercy, grace and judgment.

DESTROY THE RIGHTEOUS WITH THE WICKED: The following conversation reveals something priceless in the character of Abraham. He was in a unique relationship with God, set apart from the world around him, and it would have been easy for him to think of his own needs. However, his concern was to know God and to intercede for others. Abraham began his intercession by effectively praying that Lot would not be destroyed along with the people of Sodom.

INTERCEDING FOR SODOM: It is not surprising that Abraham intercedes for Lot's safety, but then he goes a step beyond and intercedes for the whole city.

24. SUPPOSE THERE WERE FIFTY: Abraham asked God to withhold His judgment on the city if there were righteous men living there, beginning with fifty and working his way down to ten. It is tempting to wonder what the Lord might have said if Abraham had continued down to one righteous person, but we must not lose sight of what he was doing in this conversation. Abraham was interceding on behalf of people he didn't know—people who were notoriously

wicked and had caused him personal hardship in the past (see Genesis 14). In addition, he was interceding for them with patience and diligence. In this, he is a role model for God's people of all generations.

25. FAR BE IT FROM YOU: Abraham was as concerned about the reputation of God as he was about the people of Sodom. He suggested that God's name would be smirched if He were to act in an unjust manner toward those who served Him.

SHALL NOT THE JUDGE OF ALL THE EARTH DO RIGHT: Here again, Abraham was seeking to understand the character of God. He wanted to *know* God in the same intimate way that God knew him. His rhetorical question underscored the fact that God is inherently righteous and that He will, of course, always do what is just. Abraham was also keeping a right attitude about his own station in life, as he had during the entire conversation. He was trying to imitate God in doing what was right, and this led him to intercede for his neighbors.

26. I WILL SPARE ALL THE PLACE FOR THEIR SAKES: Notice that God's response went above and beyond saving the righteous from the destruction of the wicked. God actually imputed grace to the wicked on behalf of the righteous, thus sparing the wicked as well as the righteous. What we discover in this amazing offer is that God's people can actually extend His grace to the world around them simply by their presence. This is part of what Jesus was referring to when He told His followers, "You are the salt of the earth" (Matthew 5:13). God's people are called to arrest corruption and bring healing, just as salt does—and as Lot failed to do.

27. I WHO AM BUT DUST AND ASHES: Abraham did not take his privilege for granted. God had reached out to him, permitting him the privilege of standing in His presence and speaking his mind freely, but Abraham did not forget that he was but a sinful man in the presence of the Holy Creator. Jesus made it possible for Christians to "come boldly to the throne of grace" (Hebrews 4:16), yet we also do well to remember that we are but dust. We enter God's presence by His grace, not by our merit.

32. FOR THE SAKE OF TEN: That the number of righteous people necessary to forestall judgment had been reduced from fifty to ten may have reflected Abraham's awareness both of the intense wickedness of the cities as well as Lot's ineffective witness there. Abraham probably had the whole of Lot's family in mind.

GOING DEEPER

Read James 2:17–26, noting the key words and phrases indicated below.

FAITH WITHOUT WORKS: James addresses an important aspect of the Christian life, which he calls "works." These works represent the elements of a holy life that flow from a heart of faith.

2:17. FAITH BY ITSELF: We must balance this passage with Paul's teachings in Romans 4, which we examined in study 3. James here agrees that it is faith—and faith alone—that saves us, but that we will inevitably follow saving faith with "works" of righteousness. In other words, our faith saves us and then flowers into righteous behavior.

18. YOUR FAITH WITHOUT YOUR WORKS: James emphasizes the fact that our faith in Christ will always lead to holy living: loving our neighbors, serving others, considering others as better than ourselves, and many other fruits of righteousness. A true saving faith will always lead to righteous works. We cannot have one without the other.

19. EVEN THE DEMONS BELIEVE: This is the difference between "believing" and "accepting." It is not enough to just *believe* (in terms of mere intellectual assent) that Jesus is the Son of God and that He died on the cross and rose again to save us from our sins. Even the demons believe these bare historical facts about Jesus, yet they are forever lost just the same. Rather, we must believe, *accept* His free gift of salvation, and *affirm* Him as our Lord and Savior.

ABRAHAM'S EXAMPLE: Abraham provides us with a good example of what James is discussing here because Abraham had a faith that was carried out into works.

21. JUSTIFIED BY WORKS: Abraham was declared righteous many years before Isaac was even born (see Genesis 15:6). Later, he would demonstrate his saving faith—his righteousness in the eyes of God—to the world when he obediently sacrificed Isaac (see Genesis 22). God never sends a test that His children cannot pass, and He knew that Abraham's faith would impel him to obey His command. God also knew that Abraham's saving faith would lead him to another element of

"good works": interceding for others. All of these traits of Abraham are the good works that should result from our own faith in Jesus Christ.

22. BY WORKS FAITH WAS MADE PERFECT: This is what we see happening in Genesis 18. God selected Abraham to be His representative to the world and to act as salt and light. God calls Christians for the same purpose. God, through His grace, has saved us, and He subsequently calls us to show that same grace to our neighbors. This calling is made complete, or "perfect," when our saving faith flowers and blooms into works of righteousness and love for the world around us.

23. ABRAHAM BELIEVED GOD: According to James, Abraham's faith saved him and brought him into righteousness before God. But this relationship was only "perfected" (tested and proven, brought to completion or fruition) when it led to good works in Abraham's life—interceding for others and obedience to God.

THE FRIEND OF GOD: What an amazing title! This is the very thing we saw in Genesis 18 when Abraham stood side-by-side with God, speaking to Him face-to-face as a man speaks to his friend. "No longer do I call you servants, for a servant does not know what his master is doing; but I have called you friends, for all things that I heard from My Father I have made known to you" (John 15:15).

UNLEASHING THE TEXT

1) Abraham went to great lengths and risk to rescue Lot and the people of Sodom from captivity. How might you have responded if you were in his place?

_____

_____

_____

_____

2) Why do you think Abraham stopped when he got down to ten righteous people? Why not go all the way down to one? Would it have made any difference?

_____

_____

_____

_____

_____

3) What does this conversation reveal about Abraham's character?

_____

_____

_____

_____

_____

4) What does this conversation reveal about God's character?

_____

_____

_____

_____

_____

EXPLORING THE MEANING

We are all called to be friends of God. It is easy to become complacent about this concept—to take for granted what a priceless treasure we have in our relationship with God through Christ. When we pray, we are entering freely into the presence of the Creator of the universe! This is a privilege that came at tremendous cost—the painful death of God's own Son—and we can easily forget how privileged we are.

As God's friends, we are invited to enter His presence at any time. More than this, we are *urged* to do so, for God is actually eager to fellowship with us! Abraham demonstrated the proper attitude toward this incredible blessing when he stood with God to speak as a man speaks to a friend—and then stepped even closer to speak to Him intimately. This attitude is both pleasing to God and profitable to His children.

Friendship is a two-way relationship. As we saw in the last study, God came to Abraham's home for an unexpected visit. Abraham did nothing to initiate that visit, but he did respond by welcoming the Lord and His angels with a costly feast. He did not initiate the conversation with God as the angels departed for Sodom, but he did respond by deliberately drawing closer and speaking intimately with his Creator.

We do nothing to initiate or accomplish our salvation, but we can do much to increase our intimacy with God. He already knows us intimately—better than we know ourselves—and even to the point of numbering the hairs on our heads. He also wants us to know Him intimately. This is the point where our fellowship with Him requires effort from us.

We come to know God intimately when we follow the examples of men such as Abraham, David, and other saints from Scripture. Deliberately drawing close to Him in worship, interceding for others, confessing our sins promptly and fully, and studying His Word to learn more about His character are just a few of the things that God's friends will do to deepen their friendship with Him.

We are saved by faith, but we must demonstrate that faith through good works. This is a difficult concept to grasp. There is always the danger that we will become proud of our works and think we are saved because we are special, or we may fall into legalism and believe that we must add to God's salvation by our own works. Neither of these extremes is true, yet we are still called to show forth our salvation through the works of our lives.

Abraham was found righteous in God's eyes when he believed God's promise—in spite of the fact that it was utterly impossible for him to have children. This same faith in God's promise—in God's character—would later lead him to believe that God could raise Isaac from the dead, which led him to act in faith by being willing to sacrifice his son. In this way, his faith was producing both his salvation *and* his good works, and it was by both together that his faith was proven to the world around him.

When we obey God's Word and live holy lives, the world around us will see the reality of our faith. Words alone cannot accomplish this. When we preach our faith but don't *live* by faith, we are acting no better than the devil's minions. They, too, know God's truth, but their empty belief is insufficient to save them. When we accept Christ as our Savior, we also receive the Holy Spirit into our lives, and He is faithful to produce the fruit of our salvation for all to see.

REFLECTING ON THE TEXT

5) What does it mean to be a friend of God? What does it mean to be friends with the world? Give practical examples of each.

_____

_____

_____

_____

_____

6) What things did God do to demonstrate His friendship with Abraham? What did Abraham do to deepen that friendship?

_____

_____

_____

7) What does it mean to "love your neighbor" (Mark 12:31)? How does a Christian draw a line between loving a sinner and condoning sin?

_____

_____

_____

_____

8) What is the difference between being saved by faith and being saved by good works? How do good works play a part in a Christian's life?

_____

_____

_____

_____

_____

PERSONAL RESPONSE

9) What are you doing to deepen your friendship with God? What could you do that you aren't doing now?

_____

_____

_____

_____

10) Who are the people in your life—your family, friends, neighbors, coworkers—who need your intercession? Pray for those people regularly, and let them know that you are praying for them.

_____

_____

_____

_____

7

DESTRUCTION OF SODOM AND GOMORRAH

Genesis 19:1–38

DRAWING NEAR

Life is generally filled with making compromises. What are some of the benefits of compromise that you have witnessed? What are some of the drawbacks?

_____

_____

_____

_____

THE CONTEXT

As we saw in the last study, when God visited Abraham and spoke to him face-to-face as a friend, Abraham humbly pleaded that the Lord would not bring destruction on Sodom and Gomorrah. In this action we see that Abraham not only had a unique relationship with God but also that he cared about the welfare of others. Abraham lived by faith, and that faith naturally worked itself out through his actions.

What a contrast we find in his nephew Lot. When we left him in Genesis 13, he had just been rescued by Abraham from a force led by Chedorlaomer, the king of Elam. While this should have served as a warning to Lot not to associate with wickedness, when we see him again he is even more engrained in the affairs of the wicked city of Sodom. The results, as we will discover, are disastrous not only for him but also for his family.

The reason that Lot survived at all came about as a result of Abraham's intercession on his behalf. "It came to pass, when God destroyed the cities of the plain, that God remembered Abraham, and sent Lot out of the midst of the overthrow" (Genesis 19:29). In many ways, Lot's story is similar to what we find in the account of the Flood, where God "remembered Noah" (Genesis 8:1) and caused the waters to subside. Like Noah, only Lot and his family were considered righteous in their communities, and only they were spared from God's wrath on the earth.

Lot's example is a lesson to us today to never allow ourselves to compromise with the ungodly. "For what fellowship has righteousness with lawlessness? And what communion has light with darkness?" (2 Corinthians 6:14). Lot also serves as a reminder that we must be driven by faith rather than fear, trusting that God will always deliver on what He promises, for "He who calls you is faithful, who also will do it" (1 Thessalonians 5:24). The enemy will always try to get us to accept the thinking, values, and presuppositions of the world, so we must be aware of his schemes and continually on guard against his attacks.

KEYS TO THE TEXT

Read Genesis 19:1–38, noting the key words and phrases indicated below.

> *YEARS LATER: As we have seen, Lot gave up his nomadic lifestyle entirely in favor of settling down in a fortified city. Unfortunately, his choice of retirement homes isn't too good.*

19:1. TWO ANGELS: These were the angels who, with God, had visited Abraham (see Genesis 18:22). They had taken human form.

LOT WAS SITTING IN THE GATE: This was a sign of respect and authority in the ancient world. A high wall probably surrounded the city, and the only way in and out was through a fortified gate. The elders of the city would sit in the gateway and "hold court," acting as judges for the people of the city as well as leaders and decision makers. Lot had risen to prominence in Sodom.

2. PLEASE TURN IN TO YOUR SERVANT'S HOUSE: Lot's invitation to the two angels to partake of his hospitality was most likely not only courtesy but also an effort to protect them from the known perversity of the Sodomites.

3. ENTERED HIS HOUSE: Lot was no longer living in a tent but had settled himself comfortably in Sodom. The Bible is clear that "blessed is the man who walks not in the counsel of the ungodly, nor stands in the path of sinners, nor sits in the seat of the scornful" (Psalm 1:1). Lot had, unfortunately, made this very progression by walking as a nomad toward the worldly city of Sodom, then standing together with its residents, and finally sitting in the seat of an elder of that city.

4. ALL THE PEOPLE FROM EVERY QUARTER: Before the angels even had a chance to retire for the night, word spread through the city that strangers had come to town—and virtually every male of the city flocked to Lot's door. The picture here is of men who are driven by their lusts, choosing to obey their insatiable and enslaving drives.

SURROUNDED THE HOUSE: These lustful savages had no intention of parley or even seduction; they arrived at Lot's house intent on violently taking what they wanted.

5. BRING THEM OUT TO US THAT WE MAY KNOW THEM CARNALLY: These men intended to sexually assault the angels, to forcibly indulge in homosexual carnality. Such activity, even today, is known as *sodomy*—whether done voluntarily or otherwise. God condemns every kind of homosexuality (see Leviticus 20:13 and 1 Corinthians 6:9).

LOT'S FOLLY: We now begin to see how Lot's years of following the world's priorities have turned him into a fearful and unwise old man.

7. PLEASE, MY BRETHREN: Lot demonstrated he had lost his wisdom when he tried to compromise and hold "peace talks" with these men. These wicked people were not interested in reason, truth, or compromise, but only in satisfying their desires. Eve made the same mistake when she attempted to debate theology with the Devil (see Genesis 3). It is telling that Lot referred to

these ungodly men as "my brethren." The world is not a brotherhood to God's people.

8. TWO DAUGHTERS WHO HAVE NOT KNOWN A MAN: In a shockingly misguided and unthinkable attempt to protect his angelic guests, Lot suggested that the angry mob be given his two virgin daughters.

YOU MAY DO TO THEM AS YOU WISH: What a tragic picture this presents of how far a man can sink. Lot offered his daughters to be terribly abused and probably killed by an angry mob—an entire city of men. It is tempting to see Lot as a vile man, and in this instance his actions were clearly inexcusable, yet the New Testament refers to him as "righteous Lot" (2 Peter 2:7). This is yet another demonstration of God's grace. He is able to save even the lowest of sinners.

THEY HAVE COME UNDER THE SHADOW OF MY ROOF: Ancient custom required that a man ensure the safety and comfort of guests within his house. Lot would have been deeply disgraced if the angels had come to harm while in his home. It is sad, however, that he cared more about such social customs than about protecting his daughters—who also lived under his roof.

9. HE KEEPS ACTING AS A JUDGE: These men had willingly submitted to Lot as a judge just a few hours before when he was sitting in the city gate. But this is the way of the world: when a person stands up and tells people not to be unrighteous, they turn around and accuse him of being judgmental.

10. THE MEN REACHED OUT THEIR HANDS: The angels of the Lord did not waste their time and effort trying to reason and plead with the Sodomites. This demonstrates: (1) the correct way to deal with the arguments of the world is to firmly resist them without engaging in empty debate, and (2) God's grace and mercy is immense. Lot was in this mess because of his own poor decisions, yet God came all the way to his house just to rescue him from the coming judgment.

11. BLINDNESS: The men of Sodom were already spiritually blind, and now God made them physically blind as well.

GET OUT OF TOWN: *The next morning, Lot is given strict instructions to leave town and not look back. God is extending His mercy to Lot, but he still had to obey God's commands.*

13. TAKE THEM OUT OF THIS PLACE: Lot's family should not have been in Sodom in the first place.

14. TO HIS SONS-IN-LAW HE SEEMED TO BE JOKING: Lot had apparently not indulged in the sins of Sodom, yet he had still lost his credibility among his neighbors and even his own family. This is an important principle to understand: when we live at peace with the world around us, we risk losing our testimony even if we do not indulge in worldly practices.

16. WHILE HE LINGERED: Lot was having grave difficulty leaving behind all his possessions and comfortable lifestyle. "For where your treasure is, there your heart will be also" (Matthew 6:21).

17. DO NOT LOOK BEHIND YOU: Looking back implies having second thoughts, regrets at what you have left behind in following God's commands. "No one, having put his hand to the plow, and looking back, is fit for the kingdom of God" (Luke 9:62).

ESCAPE TO THE MOUNTAINS: Lot's uncle Abraham was living in the mountains a short way to the northwest. (The angels had covered the distance in less than a day.) If Lot had immediately obeyed what the angels commanded, his final end might have been less disgraceful.

A WEE LITTLE TOWN: Lot began to let fear take control of his heart, and as a result he forgets to place his faith in the Lord—even after his miraculous rescue.

18. PLEASE, NO, MY LORDS: It is hard to believe that Lot had the audacity to argue with the Lord's command after all he had been through this day, but it speaks of his long habit of self-indulgence. There is a whining quality to his words here.

LEST SOME EVIL OVERTAKE ME AND I DIE: Lot presented a strong contrast to his uncle Abraham. He had just seen the dramatic rescue and patient grace of God in his life, but here he invented fears of what might happen if he obeyed God's further commands. Abraham, by contrast, obeyed in faith, and it was counted to him as righteousness.

20. PLEASE LET ME ESCAPE THERE (IS IT NOT A LITTLE ONE?): Again we detect a whining, wheedling tone of voice in Lot's words. He was like a spoiled child, intent on having his own way. In this he resembled the men of Sodom.

AND MY SOUL SHALL LIVE: Once again, we see that Lot had lost his trust in God's faithfulness. God had gone to great lengths to rescue Lot out of

Sodom, "the LORD being merciful to him" (Genesis 19:16), yet Lot's underlying attitude was that God was leading him into some kind of trap. *If I do exactly what the Lord commanded,* he thought, *I will be led into death and my soul shall perish.* This mindset grows as we become comfortable in the world around us because we begin to think that we have full control over our environment and our destiny. The one who lives by faith, on the other hand, is constantly reminded that he can do nothing without God's help.

> *JUDGMENT RAINS DOWN: As soon as Lot and his family are safely out of range, a dreadful cataclysm falls from the sky, destroying both Sodom and Gomorrah.*

21. I WILL NOT OVERTHROW THIS CITY FOR WHICH YOU HAVE SPO-KEN: Abraham had pleaded with God the day before to save Sodom and Gomorrah (see Genesis 18), and here we discover that it was actually God's desire to spare men from judgment. While Abraham begged for mercy for others, Lot was most concerned with his own safety. This is yet another result of making oneself comfortable in the world's system.

25. AND WHAT GREW ON THE GROUND: The area at the southern end of the Dead Sea is characterized by salt and blasted rock. It is not conducive to supporting natural life.

26. HIS WIFE LOOKED BACK: The angels had specifically warned Lot to not look back as they were fleeing, but Lot's wife disregarded this command. As a result she not only became encased in salt but also served as a poignant example of disobedience producing unwanted reaction at Judgment Day (see Luke 17:29–32), even as her home cities became bywords of God's judgment on sin (see Romans 9:29; 2 Peter 2:5–6).

> *LOT'S SHAMEFUL END: Lot's fear became his motivating force toward the end of his days, and he once again lost his trust in the Lord. This sad story is the last we hear of him in the Old Testament.*

30. HE WAS AFRAID TO DWELL IN ZOAR: This may be because Lot felt the people in Zoar would blame him for the nearby devastation or because Lot himself was afraid that further destruction might come to the surrounding

areas. In either case, we again see Lot motivated by fear rather than by faith. This is in direct contrast to the confidence in God that characterized his uncle Abraham.

31. THERE IS NO MAN ON THE EARTH TO COME IN TO US: Now we find that Lot's daughters suffered from fear just as their father did. They persuaded themselves that there was "no man on the earth" for them to marry—a rather absurd conclusion, as though the destruction of Sodom and Gomorrah had annihilated the entire earth and all its inhabitants. Once again, we see how fear leads God's people into trouble, not into His arms. Fear is a lack of faith.

37–38. MOABITES ... PEOPLE OF AMMON: The Moabites and Ammonites became two of Israel's fiercest and most persistent enemies. Lot's flirtation with the world—concluding with the incestuous immorality of his daughters—ultimately led to suffering and warfare for God's people for many generations to come.

GOING DEEPER

Read 2 Peter 2:4–11, noting the key words and phrases indicated below.

> THREE JUDGMENTS: *Peter uses the story of God's judgment against Sodom and Gomorrah to show how God will one day judge those who spread the lies and false teachings of the enemy.*

2:4. GOD DID NOT SPARE: Peter gives three powerful illustrations of past divine judgment on the wicked to show how God will ultimately judge the wicked false teachers of his day. These illustrations set the precedents for the future and final judgment on liars and deceivers.

THE ANGELS WHO SINNED: This was a judgment against the fallen angels of Genesis 6, who left their normal state and lusted after women. These permanently bound demons are like prisoners who are incarcerated awaiting final sentencing.

5. DID NOT SPARE THE ANCIENT WORLD: This refers to the judgment on the ancient world through the worldwide Flood (see Genesis 6–8). The human race was reduced to eight people by that judgment.

6. SODOM AND GOMORRAH: The third precedent for a future divine judgment on the wicked is the total destruction of Sodom and Gomorrah and the surrounding cities. As we have seen, this judgment destroyed every person in the area by incineration.

MAKING THEM AN EXAMPLE: God sent an unmistakable message to all future generations that wickedness results in judgment.

> ONE RIGHTEOUS MAN: *Even though Lot had his failings, God called him righteous and delivered him from the destruction on Sodom and Gomorrah.*

7. DELIVERED RIGHTEOUS LOT: Lot was righteous, as all the saved are, by faith in the true God. Righteousness was imputed to him by grace through faith, as it was to Abraham. In both of the illustrations where God rendered a wholesale judgment on all living people (once on the whole earth, and once in the region of the plain south of the Dead Sea), God's people were rescued.

OPPRESSED BY THE FILTHY CONDUCT OF THE WICKED: There was spiritual weakness in Lot, yet he did hate the sins of his culture and sought ways to protect God's angels from harm. The Greek word for "oppressed" implies that he was troubled deeply and tortured with the immoral, outrageous behavior of the people living in and around Sodom and Gomorrah. Tragically, it is ordinary for believers to be no longer shocked by the rampant sin in today's society.

9. TO RESERVE THE UNJUST: The wicked are kept like prisoners awaiting the sentencing that will send them to their eternal prison.

UNLEASHING THE TEXT

1) Unlike Abraham, Lot had given up his nomadic lifestyle and settled himself in the city of Sodom. How did that affect his wisdom and decision-making?

_____

_____

_____

_____

2) In what ways had Lot lost his credibility with his neighbors and his own family? In what ways had he lost his trust in God?

_____

_____

_____

_____

3) Why did God decide to destroy Sodom and Gomorrah in the first place? Was He justified in doing so?

_____

_____

_____

_____

4) How did Lot end up committing incest with his daughters? What steps led him to that situation, beginning with his separation from Abraham?

_____

_____

_____

_____

Exploring the Meaning

God does not condone sexual perversion, including the so-called "gay life-style." God's judgment fell on Sodom because the people of that city had given themselves over to sexual perversion and other forms of self-indulgence. The Bible warns again and again that those who indulge in sexual immorality will not inherit the kingdom of God (for example, see 1 Corinthians 6:9).

The world today teaches that sexual immorality is actually acceptable, normal, and even healthy. In fact, the concept of "immorality" itself has all but disappeared from the thinking of the common man. Even the definition of marriage itself is under attack from the world today. Yet God is emphatic that any form of sexual intercourse outside the sacred bonds of marriage is considered immoral and destructive. This includes fornication, adultery, homosexuality, and any other sexual activity that is not between a man and his wife.

We must not allow ourselves to be deceived by the lies of the world in this matter. God's people are absolutely forbidden to engage in sexual activity apart from the bonds of marriage, regardless of what nice-sounding names the world may give to those activities. The history of Sodom stands as a solemn warning on how seriously the Lord takes these matters.

The teachings of the world can corrupt the thinking of even God's people. Lot demonstrated this concept in the way he interacted with the lust-driven maniacs of Sodom. A mob of rapists assailed his door, and he stepped outside and tried to reason with the crowd. He tried to appeal to their sense of goodness and propriety—even though they had none. He even went so far as to offer his own virgin daughters to be raped to death by the madmen. Lot was also driven by fear rather than faith—fear he invented for himself that had no basis in reality.

These are examples of how his thinking had been corrupted by the philosophies of Sodom. He had come to believe that the godly must compromise with the ungodly, that reason and logic could overcome the lust of the flesh, and that God would not protect him even after He had promised to do so. It is not surprising that the world instills these same attitudes in Christians today.

In Romans 12:2, Paul writes, "Do not be conformed to this world, but be transformed by the renewing of your mind, that you may prove what is that good and acceptable and perfect will of God" (Romans 12:1–2). Lot had "conformed" or assumed an outward expression based on the culture that did not reflect what was really inside. As believers, we are rather to be "transformed" and outwardly display our inner, redeemed natures.

God's judgment will come to the wicked. The greatest sin of Christ-rejecters and the most damning work of Satan is misrepresentation of the truth and its consequent deception. Nothing is more wicked than for someone to claim to speak for God to the salvation of souls when, in reality, he speaks for Satan to the damnation of souls. In Peter's day, these types of individuals were parading themselves as Christian pastors, teachers, and evangelists. Peter makes it clear that "their judgment has not been idle, and their destruction does not slumber" (2 Peter 2:3).

The example of the destruction of Sodom and Gomorrah shows that while God is merciful and extends opportunities for people to change their immoral ways, a time will come when His judgment will fall. Though God takes "no pleasure in the death of the wicked" (Ezekiel 33:11), He must judge wickedness because His holiness requires it.

The wicked are like prisoners awaiting the sentencing that will send them to their eternal prison. Their final judgment will be the Great White Throne judgment (see Revelation 20:11–15), where all the ungodly of all the ages will be raised, judged finally, and cast into the lake of fire.

REFLECTING ON THE TEXT

5) What does the world teach concerning homosexuality? How do those teachings compare with the Bible's teachings? How do you respond to this conflict?

_____

_____

_____

_____

_____

6) Second Peter 2:7–8 tells us that Lot was a righteous man. How do you reconcile that with his choices and actions in Genesis 19? How can a righteous man sink to such depths?

_____

_____

_____

_____

_____

7) When have you discovered that the world's values or presuppositions have worked their way into your own attitudes? How did you correct your thinking?

_____

_____

_____

_____

_____

8) When have you seen an unexpected side effect of your own actions in someone else's life with bad results? When have you seen it with good results?

_____

_____

_____

PERSONAL RESPONSE

9) What comforts of the world threaten to interfere with your own Christian walk? What needs to change in your life to guard against this danger?

_____

_____

_____

_____

10) In your own mind, what are the areas of sexual purity with which you face the greatest struggle or temptation? What does God's Word say about those sins? How can His Word strengthen you this week?

_____

_____

_____

_____

8

THE BIRTH OF ISAAC

Genesis 21:1–21

DRAWING NEAR

In today's reading, Abraham was required to trust God with the welfare of his son Ishmael. Why is it especially difficult for parents to release control when it comes to their children? What fears do they have when it comes to taking a step back?

_____

_____

_____

_____

_____

THE CONTEXT

At long last God's promised son was born to Abraham and Sarah, ending the twenty-five years of waiting and suspense. The barrenness of Sarah was over, and her earlier laughter of derision had turned to rejoicing. She named the boy Isaac, which literally means "he laughs," and anticipated that her joy would be universally shared.

But this would not be the case, for the birth of Isaac now meant that Abraham's son through Hagar would no longer be his sole heir. As so often happens, one person's joy proved to be the source of another's jealousy, and Ishmael started to mock Isaac's status. This led Sarah—the one who had persuaded her husband to stop waiting for God and have the child with Hagar in the first place—to call for them to be cast out.

Sarah, like her husband, was a very real human being, and Scripture records her foibles and failures just as much as her victories and joy. Yet while she was far from perfect, the New Testament points to her as a woman of great character, worthy of our emulation today. It may come as a surprise in our modern day of "liberated women" to discover that she never headed up a corporation or ran for president. In fact, Peter points to her as an example of godly womanhood specifically because of her quiet and gentle spirit—and her behind-the-scenes role in the life of her husband (see 1 Peter 3:6).

In this study, we will take a closer look at this great woman, how God fulfilled His promise through the birth of Isaac, and how He ultimately provided for Hagar and Ishmael. In the process, we will examine what we as modern Christians can learn from the example of Abraham and Sarah—a couple who was significant in the line of Christ—and how God orchestrates events to accomplish His will on earth.

KEYS TO THE TEXT

Read Genesis 21:1–21, noting the key words and phrases indicated below.

> *MIRACLE BIRTH: Within a year of God's visit to Abraham (see Genesis 18), Sarah gave birth to Isaac—just as the Lord had promised. It had taken some twenty-five years, but at last the Lord's promise had come to pass.*

21:3. ISAAC: God had directed Abraham to bestow this name on his son after Abraham laughed in disbelief at God's promise (see Genesis 17:19). The name became doubly appropriate when Sarah laughed in the same manner. It would now commemorate a more joyful laughter than these brief episodes of doubt on the part of the boy's parents.

4. ABRAHAM CIRCUMCISED HIS SON ISAAC: This rite of circumcision was immensely important prior to the time of Christ, because it was the outward display of a man's commitment to Jehovah. This ties together with what we considered in study 6—the combination of faith and works in the life of a Christian. Circumcision was the outward display of one's faith, even as obedience and good works are the outward display of a Christian's faith.

5. ABRAHAM WAS ONE HUNDRED YEARS OLD: Sarah was ninety.

SON OF LAUGHER: Now, at last, Sarah's faith is rewarded, her righteousness is made evident to the world around her, and her laughter is made joyful.

6. GOD HAS MADE ME LAUGH: Sarah's derisive, mocking laughter had been turned to joy. "Sing, O barren, you who have not borne! Break forth into singing, and cry aloud, you who have not labored with child! For more are the children of the desolate than the children of the married woman" (Isaiah 54:1).

ALL WHO HEAR: This brings us back to the basic reason that God chose Abraham and Sarah for this purpose: they were to be beacons to the world around them, demonstrating God's grace and showing the nations what it meant to be a follower of Jehovah. Sarah realized that the world was watching, and in this glorious moment her faith was vindicated.

7. WHO WOULD HAVE SAID TO ABRAHAM THAT SARAH WOULD NURSE CHILDREN: Sarah was expressing her unmixed wonder at God's miraculous fulfillment—a birth (and subsequent nursing) that was physically impossible. Yet her words also incriminated her to a degree for the simple reason that God Himself had told Abraham that Sarah would nurse children! God's Word always comes to pass, and He never fails to keep His promises. Never.

8. WEANED: This usually occurred in the second or third year.

MOCKING THE HEIR: Ishmael was probably about fifteen years older than Isaac, approximately seventeen at the time Isaac was weaned. He was not a gracious older brother.

9. THE SON OF HAGAR: Ishmael.

10. SHALL NOT BE HEIR WITH MY SON: This was what God told Abraham in the first place (see Genesis 15:3–4; 17:18–20). Sarah's plan accomplished

nothing good—as the couple found themselves back where they had been in the first place—but it did accomplish much that was *not* good.

11. THE MATTER WAS VERY DISPLEASING IN ABRAHAM'S SIGHT: In other words, this time Abraham refused to heed his wife's counsel.

12. LISTEN TO HER VOICE: However, this time Abraham also sought the Lord's will and, ironically, discovered that his wife's advice was in accordance with God's plan. The difference lay in the fact that Abraham sought the Lord's will and took his proper role as spiritual head of the household.

13. I WILL ALSO MAKE A NATION OF THE SON OF THE BONDWOMAN: Ishmael's descendants include many of the modern Arabic nations. There has always been grievous enmity between them and Israel, and the descendants of Isaac have suffered greatly from the descendants of Ishmael.

14. SENT HER AWAY: This seems horribly heartless, yet we must remember that this situation would never have arisen in the first place if Abraham and Sarah had not tried to take matters into their own hands with Hagar. God had made it abundantly clear that His promise would be fulfilled through Isaac alone and that He would not tolerate any adulteration of His chosen seed. As we will see in the New Testament, it was essential that Ishmael be sent away from Isaac, for Isaac alone was the chosen heir of Abraham. Ishmael could not share that inheritance.

GOD HEARS ISHMAEL: *Hagar and Ishmael wander into the desert and soon run out of water. Hagar goes a distance away so she will not see her son die. But God has other plans.*

WILDERNESS OF BEERSHEBA: A wide, extensive desert on the southern border of Israel.

17. GOD HEARD THE VOICE OF THE LAD: When desperation turned Ishmael's scoffing into a cry of anguish at probable death from thirst, God heard him. Years before, God had also heard Hagar's cries when she had run away from Sarah.

ANGEL OF GOD: Literally "messenger of Yahweh" who, in context, turns out to be the Lord Himself.

I WILL MAKE HIM A GREAT NATION: Here God was reiterating a promise he had previously made to Hagar: "As for Ishmael, I have heard you. Behold,

I have blessed him, and will make him fruitful, and will multiply him exceedingly. He shall beget twelve princes, and I will make him a great nation" (Genesis 17:20).

21. WILDERNESS OF PARAN: This was located in the northeast section of the Sinai peninsula, the area called Arabia.

GOING DEEPER

Read 1 Peter 3:1–12, noting the key words and phrases indicated below.

> *BE SUBMISSIVE: Previously Abraham had put himself under the spiritual authority of his wife, and this led to the current problem with Hagar and Ishmael. In this passage, Peter discusses why it is so important for husbands to exert spiritual leadership in the home.*

3:1. LIKEWISE: Peter, in the previous chapter of his letter, had expounded on the fact that Christians are called to be submissive to Christ and to one another. Now he carries this doctrine into the home, urging wives to submit to the spiritual leadership of their husbands and husbands to show honor to their wives.

BE SUBMISSIVE TO YOUR OWN HUSBANDS: This doctrine goes across the grain in modern Western society, but Christians are called upon to obey the Word of God, not the teachings of the world around us. The Greek word translated "submissive" is a compound word, meaning to "rank under." It means that the wife should voluntarily consider herself to be under the rank, or authority, of her husband—to consider him as outranking her. Notice how Peter qualified this: "submissive to your *own* husbands." This underscores the fact that a woman is not inferior to a man any more than one Christian is inferior to another. Peter was addressing roles within *marriage* and calling the wife to consider herself as "outranked" by her husband—but not by other men.

EVEN IF SOME DO NOT OBEY THE WORD: This teaching applies to wives whose husbands are not Christians as well as those whose husbands obey the Word of God. This hierarchy of authority goes back to Creation, before mankind even fell into sin.

A QUIET WITNESS: A Christian woman can actually lead her unsaved husband to Christ—without speaking a word. This is done by submission.

MAY BE WON BY THE CONDUCT OF THEIR WIVES: A submissive Christian wife may compel her unbelieving husband toward Christ by the simple example of her obedience to God's Word. This is accomplished "without a word," Peter says, because actions speak louder than words. A wife's example of submission to her husband is an example of being submissive to Christ, and this example alone—without any unnecessary preaching—is enough to demonstrate the reality of her faith. The loving, gracious submission of a Christian woman to her unsaved husband is the strongest evangelistic tool she has.

2. WHEN THEY OBSERVE: The word translated "observe" means "to view attentively." Peter was suggesting that the unsaved husband would be watching his wife closely to see how well she lived out her faith—and how well her faith worked in her life. This ties back to Sarah's comment, "God has made me laugh, and all who hear will laugh with me" (Genesis 21:6).

CHASTE CONDUCT ACCOMPANIED BY FEAR: Fear in the sense of reverence—both toward God and toward her husband.

HIDDEN PERSON OF THE HEART: We are not to spend time worrying about our outward appearance; it is the inner person that matters.

3. DO NOT LET YOUR ADORNMENT BE MERELY OUTWARD: Peter was not condemning outward adornments or a woman's desire to make herself presentable or even stylish. He was warning against allowing that to become a preoccupation or obsession—a danger that is very real in our modern culture. A Christian's focus should be on the inner person—and this doctrine applies just as much to men as to women.

4. THE HIDDEN PERSON OF THE HEART: The word "hidden" comes from *cryptos,* from which we get our English words "cryptic" and "encryption." It implies a secret, such as the encryption that is used to keep computer data from being stolen. The hidden person of the heart is the deepest, secret, inner person—the "real you" that only God can fully know.

INCORRUPTIBLE BEAUTY: A woman's beauty will generally fade as she ages, but a godly woman's inner beauty will increase as she grows in the likeness of Christ. Once again this ties back to Sarah in the sense that her body had aged beyond the ability to produce or nurse a baby, but God miraculously brought forth a deeper, more lasting beauty in her old age.

GENTLE AND QUIET SPIRIT: The gentleness refers to meekness and humility, a gentleness of spirit. The quiet spirit is one that is not easily ruffled—either by circumstances or by a husband who is difficult to get along with. These qualities are "very precious in the sight of God."

SARAH'S EXAMPLE: Sarah serves as the example of a godly, submissive wife.

6. CALLING HIM LORD: It is interesting that Peter should point to this instance in Genesis 18:12, since Sarah was actually voicing her doubts as to whether God could keep His promise. Yet the Lord remembered her faith, not her doubts. It can be difficult at times to cling to our trust of God's Word when circumstances go against us, and this can certainly be true for a woman's submission to an ungodly husband. But the Lord strengthens our doubts and builds our faith each time we act in faith and obedience.

WHOSE DAUGHTERS YOU ARE: We become sons of Abraham and daughters of Sarah when we act in faith and obey God's Word.

NOT AFRAID WITH ANY TERROR: We have seen numerous times in Abraham's life where fear led him away from God rather than toward faith. There are potential fears for a Christian woman who sets out to be submissive to her unsaved husband, such as whether that submission will lead toward God's will or away from it. Peter's injunction to submit to an ungodly husband, however, does not include any coercion to sin or disobey God's Word; nor does it require physical harm (compare Acts 5:28–29).

HUSBANDS: Men are called on to submit to their wives—in fact, they are called to the more difficult task of loving their wives as Christ loved the church.

7. HUSBANDS, LIKEWISE: Husbands are also called to be humble and submissive (see Ephesians 5:21), although the role of submission is different

from that of the wife. The husband is the spiritual head of the home, yet he is to lead by example rather than by tyranny. A man who desires a loving, gentle wife must demonstrate how to be loving and gentle himself.

UNDERSTANDING: This word in the Greek is *gnosis,* meaning knowledge. A cult arose in the early church (which has resurfaced in modern times under the guise of science) that taught that a person needed some "higher knowledge" if he was to fully understand God's Word. Yet here Peter touched on the *true* higher knowledge to which every Christian is called: the knowledge of love and patience toward others. A godly husband must submit himself to the task of learning to love and understand his wife, deliberately subordinating his needs to hers—whether she is a Christian or not. Peter specifically noted consideration, chivalry, and companionship.

HONOR: Showing deference and reverence.

HEIRS TOGETHER OF THE GRACE OF LIFE: Man and woman together complete the image of God (see Genesis 1:27). The "grace of life" here is not salvation but marriage. The husband must cultivate companionship and fellowship with his wife.

THAT YOUR PRAYERS MAY NOT BE HINDERED: A Christian man must love his wife as Christ loved the church (see Ephesians 5:25), setting her needs above his own. If he does not, Peter warned, his very prayers will be hindered (see Matthew 5:23–24).

UNLEASHING THE TEXT

1) Put yourself in Ishmael's place. Why might he have persecuted Isaac, who was only an infant at the time?

_____

_____

_____

_____

_____

2) Why did Sarai insist that Hagar and Ishmael be sent away? Why did God command Abraham to do so?

_____

_____

_____

_____

_____

3) How does Sarah's faith in God's promises compare with Abraham's faith?

_____

_____

_____

_____

4) In what ways does the birth of Isaac prefigure the birth of Christ?

_____

_____

_____

_____

EXPLORING THE MEANING

The man is the head of the Christ-centered home. This teaching is hard for many of us in the church, because our modern feminist culture spurns the concept of "gender roles." Feminists would shriek in disdain if told that a husband "outranks" the wife in the spiritual leadership of the home—yet this is precisely what Peter (and other biblical writers) would have us accept.

This teaching can be even more frightening for a Christian who is married to an unbeliever. It is no accident that Peter addressed both of these topics in the same passage; he made it clear that a wife's submission to her husband applies whether the husband is a Christian or not.

The reason for this is that when a woman submits herself to her husband's headship, she is indirectly submitting herself to Christ's headship. Even if that husband is not a believer, the wife will bring honor to God by submitting to the divinely ordained structure of authority for the home. There is no safer or better place for anyone to be than in direct submission to Christ.

God's people must submit to one another. This principle is closely related to the previous one and applies throughout the church, regardless of one believer's relationship to another. But once again, it is a teaching that is unpopular in our culture, which teaches that "submission" is essentially the same as slavery. This is the opposite of what Scripture teaches; God's Word makes it clear that a Christian can never know true freedom in Christ until he or she has learned to humbly serve others.

Paul addressed this same issue regarding wives submitting to their husbands, but he prefaced that passage with the admonition that God's people should be "submitting to one another in the fear of God" (Ephesians 5:21). Elsewhere he tells us, "Let nothing be done through selfish ambition or conceit, but in lowliness of mind let each esteem others better than himself. Let each of you look out not only for his own interests, but also for the interests of others" (Philippians 2:3–4).

Submission actually has little to do with authority and everything to do with godliness. It is a voluntary act—a deliberate decision to put someone else's needs before our own. In making this decision, we are becoming imitators of Christ.

Nothing is impossible for God. Imagine how Sarah must have felt, even at age sixty-five when God first appeared to Abraham, to hear that the Lord was going to give her a child. Imagine further how she must have felt when twenty-five years went past without any pregnancy. Now imagine how Mary must have felt when an angel told her that she was already pregnant—and she was still a virgin (see Luke 1:26–38)!

The Lord deliberately waited until it was painfully clear that a birth was impossible both for Sarah and for Mary. And then He gave them sons! This was done, in part, to prove beyond any doubt that the children were miracles of God and that no man could lay any claim to having engineered that miracle.

God still calls His children to exercise total faith in Him and the promises of His Word—no matter how difficult the circumstances may seem. Perhaps He has asked you to do something that seems impossible—remain with an unsaved spouse, for example—and you just can't see how He can ever work it for His glory. But nothing is impossible for God, and He is always faithful to His promises and to His children. When He asks us to do the impossible, our job is to obey and then trust Him with the outcome. Those who put their faith and hope in God will not be disappointed.

Reflecting on the Text

5) Abraham and Sarah had real doubts about God's promise, and they even committed serious sin out of that doubt. Why did God still fulfill the promise? What does this show about His character? About His promises?

_____

_____

_____

_____

_____

6) Why did the Lord take so long to fulfill His promise of a son for Abraham and Sarah? Why did He wait until pregnancy and childrearing were so utterly impossible by human standards?

_____

_____

_____

_____

7) Why was it necessary for Ishmael to be sent away from Isaac? What provision did God make for Hagar and Ishmael? What does that tell us about God's character and His will in regard to His chosen heir for Abraham?

_____

_____

_____

_____

8) In what ways did Abraham exhibit the proper spiritual authority in this story? Why does God expect a woman to submit to her husband's authority? How does this teaching correspond with society's views?

_____

_____

_____

_____

_____

PERSONAL RESPONSE

9) How do you feel about the teachings concerning a woman's submission to her husband? If you are married, how does your marriage address this? If you are single, what sort of marriage do you desire?

_____

_____

_____

_____

10) What does Sarah's life teach us about trusting in God and His promises? How will her example help you the next time you encounter a situation that you believe to be impossible?

_____

_____

_____

_____

9

ABRAHAM'S FAITH CONFIRMED
Genesis 22:1–19

DRAWING NEAR

God often puts challenges in our lives in order to build our faith in Him. What is one situation you have experienced that stretched your faith? What was it like for you to go through that particular challenge?

_____

_____

_____

_____

THE CONTEXT

We now move ahead and revisit Abraham after the birth of his promised son, Isaac. While it is not entirely clear just how much time has passed, and while we don't know exactly how old Abraham and Isaac were when the events of Genesis 22 take place, it seems likely that Isaac was somewhere between the ages of fourteen and twenty-one. This means that Abraham was well over one hundred years old.

Abraham, Sarah, and Isaac were evidently living in Beersheba at this point, along with the many people in Abraham's extended household. Abraham had

109

undoubtedly been taking great delight in the company of his son, teaching him in the ways of the Lord and preparing him to take over as head of the great household one day.

There is a unique bond that develops between a father and his son, and this relationship is the centerpiece in the passage that we will look at in this study. A son carries on his father's name and his father's goals and aspirations. A father is eager to pass on his knowledge and wisdom to his son. For Abraham, this bond was even more significant because Isaac was the son whom had long been promised by God, and it was through Isaac that God's greater promises of a great nation of descendants would be fulfilled. Furthermore, because Abraham was well advanced in years, there was no possibility, from a human perspective, that he would ever have another child.

So imagine how shocked Abraham must have been one day when God suddenly appeared to him and told him to put his son Isaac to death! Isaac, the very son whom God had promised for so many years, the one through whom Abraham was to produce a great nation that would be more numerous than the stars (see Genesis 15:5)! How could God's promise come to pass if Isaac died so young?

Yet God's purposes are always bigger than we can understand, and there are occasions when He calls His people to do things that make no logical sense to our finite minds. At such times, we must imitate Abraham: trust and obey.

KEYS TO THE TEXT

Read Genesis 22:1–19, noting the key words and phrases indicated below.

A FINAL EXAM: Abraham's promised son has finally arrived, and Isaac is growing up. Suddenly, God comes to Abraham with the most difficult test of his life.

22:1. GOD TESTED ABRAHAM: The Hebrew word for "tested" is used of assaying metals. God was testing the quality and strength of Abraham's faith, just as a metallurgist tests the purity and temper of gold.

2. YOUR SON, YOUR ONLY SON ISAAC, WHOM YOU LOVE: Notice the strong reiterations of love and costliness in this phrase: "your son"; "your only

son"; "whom you love." It is as though the Lord was letting Abraham know that He understood just how painful and costly this would be. Indeed, this is precisely what the Lord was doing, because He Himself would one day undergo the same torture—and His Son would actually go through with the sacrifice.

THE LAND OF MORIAH: This is probably the same Mount Moriah in Jerusalem where Solomon would later build the temple (see 2 Chronicles 3:1). It is a significant landmark, a place where the Lord repeatedly revealed Himself to His people, where the Jews would worship and sacrifice for hundreds of years. Today, this site is occupied by the Dome of the Rock, a Muslim temple that encloses a large outcropping of natural stone—which is still claimed as the site of Abraham's intended sacrifice of Isaac.

OFFER HIM THERE AS A BURNT OFFERING: This command would be startling enough in any circumstances, but in Abraham's case it was doubly so: the loss of Isaac would mean that God's promise of innumerable heirs—more than the sand of the seashore—would be cut short and fail. Yet, as we will see, Abraham was so convinced of God's faithfulness to His promise that he knew Isaac could not be permanently taken away from him.

ABRAHAM'S RESPONSE: God's command makes no logical sense— how could His promise come to pass if Abraham obeys? Yet this is exactly what Abraham does.

3. SO ABRAHAM: It is interesting that Sarah does not appear in this historical account. We must resist the modern temptation of suggesting that she is omitted because of some male chauvinism on the part of Moses, as though he didn't think that a woman's perspective mattered. She does not appear in this account because the Holy Spirit was motivating Moses on what to include and exclude, and His purpose was to give us not only an account of a historical event but also a picture of an event that is yet to come—the sacrifice of the Son of God—the final sacrifice for sin—by His own Father.

ABRAHAM ROSE EARLY IN THE MORNING: When God calls us to do something that is difficult or costly, it is always best to set about obeying as quickly as possible.

HE SPLIT THE WOOD FOR THE BURNT OFFERING: The area around Jerusalem, the most likely site of Moriah, was probably wooded during the time of

Abraham. It might seem odd that he would carry split firewood for a three-day journey if he could have collected it there, but Abraham was not permitting himself any opportunity for a change of heart. Further, Abraham's advance preparations remind us of the fact that God began preparing to sacrifice His own Son on the day when Adam sinned—indeed, before the very foundation of the world.

4. ON THE THIRD DAY: God had commanded Abraham to travel to a distant mountain for the sacrifice, which at first glance seems odd since there were plenty of high places near Beersheba where he was living. Yet one part of God's reason may well be the fact that it would require a three-day journey to get there, thereby providing a picture of the death and resurrection of Christ. It is also significant that this location would one day be the place where Abraham's descendants would build the temple—a place where sacrifices took place continually.

ARRIVING AT MORIAH: After three days' travel, Abraham and Isaac arrive at the place of sacrifice. The moment of truth is at hand for Abraham.

ABRAHAM LIFTED HIS EYES: Here we see this important phrase again, which we first noted when Lot "lifted his eyes" and looked on the good things that the world had to offer (see Genesis 13:10). In stark contrast to Lot, Abraham lifted his eyes and looked on the horrific sacrifice that lay before him. In the same way, the Lord Himself would later "set His face like flint" as He went to Jerusalem to be offered up in sacrifice (see Isaiah 50:7 and Luke 9:51).

5. THE LAD AND I WILL GO: This sacrifice was intimately and solely between father and son, and nobody else was invited to participate. In the same way, the final sacrifice of God's own Son was provided and paid solely by God Himself. No man could offer any element of the atonement.

WE WILL COME BACK TO YOU: Here again we see the absolute faith and confidence that Abraham was placing in God. He knew that God would certainly fulfill His promise to make a great nation out of Isaac and was therefore completely confident that he would return again with his son. Yet he was also anticipating that he would have to put his son to death. Through absolute faith in God's promise, he was "concluding that God [was] able to raise [Isaac] up, even from the dead" (Hebrews 11:19).

Climbing Mount Moriah: The parallels between Isaac and Jesus now become startling as the son of promise climbs the mount to be offered up in sacrifice.

6. LAID IT ON ISAAC HIS SON: The father laid the burden on the shoulders of his son, just as God the Father would later do with His Son: "The LORD has laid on Him the iniquity of us all" (Isaiah 53:6). Isaac also typifies Christ in a much more literal way, as he carried the very wood that was to devour his body in sacrifice, even as Christ carried His own cross to Calvary (see John 19:17).

HE TOOK THE FIRE IN HIS HAND, AND A KNIFE: These two symbols of God's wrath forcibly remind us of the reason why a sacrifice was necessary in the first place: God's wrath and judgment against man's sin had to be appeased. Jesus bore the full brunt of God's justice as He hung on the cross, and His Father struck Him dead with His own hand. Imagine the emotions that must have surged through Abraham's breast as he carried in his own hand the very weapons he was about to use against his son. This picture can help us understand a small portion of what it cost God—Father and Son—to pay for our sins.

THE TWO OF THEM WENT TOGETHER: Isaac most likely had at least a suspicion of what his father had in mind and may well have divined his intentions fairly thoroughly. Yet he made no struggle at all and walked with his father in complete unity. In this we again see a picture of the person of Jesus, God's only begotten Son, who walked in perfect unity with the Father all the way to the cross.

WHERE IS THE LAMB: It would appear that Abraham had told Isaac little, if anything, of his intentions. In this Isaac differs from the Lord Jesus, who was fully aware of what His Father's purpose was in sending Him into the world. Yet even Isaac appeared to have at least a glimmer of what was coming, and like Christ he made no complaint.

7. ISAAC SPOKE TO ABRAHAM HIS FATHER: Isaac, being much younger than Abraham, could easily have resisted his father's intentions had he chosen to do so. Yet Isaac asked about his father's plans only once and then complied without any further comment. This picture, once again, was completed in Christ who prayed, "Father, if it is Your will, take this cup away from Me; nevertheless not My will, but Yours, be done" (Luke 22:42).

8. GOD WILL PROVIDE FOR HIMSELF THE LAMB FOR A BURNT OF-FERING: The presence of a sacrificial lamb, which served as a substitute for Isaac, again typifies the substitutionary sacrifice of Christ, who died in the place of sinners who deserved to die. This statement also demonstrates the fullness of Abraham's faith.

9. ABRAHAM BUILT AN ALTAR: Once again we see Abraham building an altar to the Lord—but this time his sacrifice and worship would be extremely costly to himself. This is the ultimate act of worship: to sacrifice something that is very precious out of obedience to God and faith in His promises. A life-time of practice in building altars and worshiping God had prepared Abraham for this fateful moment.

HE BOUND ISAAC HIS SON AND LAID HIM ON THE ALTAR: Picture this scene in your mind as a man who is more than one hundred years old attempts to tie up a youth in his late teens or early twenties. It is left to our imaginations to picture the anguish that Abraham must have been feeling at this moment—yet even this agony could not compare with what the Father would one day endure when His Son was crucified.

10. ABRAHAM STRETCHED OUT HIS HAND AND TOOK THE KNIFE TO SLAY HIS SON: What a dramatic moment! Abraham demonstrated to the ut-termost his absolute determination to obey God, even to the point of sacri-ficing his own son. His obedience and faith provide a complete picture of the sacrifice of God's Son on the cross and offer another confirmation of the truth of the Gospels—that Jesus is indeed the Messiah and the only begotten Son of God. We would have been deprived of this Old Testament picture if Abraham had balked at any point in his obedience or obeyed only partially, as he had done at previous times in his life.

STOP! Suddenly God intervenes to hold Abraham back from the final act of sacrifice. Abraham has passed his final test, providing a stunning portrait of Christ's future sufferings.

12. NOW I KNOW THAT YOU FEAR GOD: God's purposes in our lives have many facets, and we cannot know fully what He intends. Here we discover that part of God's purpose in this test was to prove, once and for all, the complete extent of Abraham's devotion to Him. We also know that God intended this

test to be a picture of His final redemption to come, though Abraham was not told this. Our place is to trust and obey, even when we cannot see God's purposes in life's circumstances.

YOU HAVE NOT WITHHELD YOUR SON: Abraham demonstrated through his actions that his love and reverence for God superseded even his deepest human relationships. Moreover, as a picture of Christ, this statement looks forward to the fact that God would not withhold His only Son in redeeming mankind from sin. "Greater love has no one than this, than to lay down one's life for his friends" (John 15:13). "For God so loved the world that He gave His only begotten Son, that whoever believes in Him should not perish but have everlasting life" (John 3:16).

13. ABRAHAM LIFTED HIS EYES: Once again we encounter this meaningful phrase, and this time Abraham's eyes beheld that which filled his heart with joy—a direct contrast to the last time he "lifted his eyes" and beheld the coming death of his son. Now he discovered that God had provided a sacrifice to take Isaac's place, and we can be assured that Abraham's heart was filled with overwhelming relief.

A BURNT OFFERING INSTEAD OF HIS SON: The truth God is demonstrating here is that no man can offer a sacrifice that will atone for his own sins—never mind the sins of others. If we are to be forgiven, our sins must be paid by a perfect substitute. Only Christ's perfect sacrifice could accomplish that—the final sacrifice God Himself provided for mankind. Jesus gave Himself as that sacrifice, dying on the cross in our place to pay the final price for our sins.

REITERATING THE PROMISE: With a covenant that can never be broken, God once again swears that He will make Abraham's descendants into a great nation.

14. THE-LORD-WILL-PROVIDE: As we have seen, this is a lesson that Abraham had to learn in his own life. Previously, he had attempted to provide for himself an heir—with disastrous results—rather than waiting for God to provide the fulfillment to His promises. "And my God shall supply all your need according to His riches in glory by Christ Jesus" (Philippians 4:19).

IN THE MOUNT OF THE LORD IT SHALL BE PROVIDED: The Mount of the Lord refers to Mount Zion in Jerusalem, the center of Jewish worship. This promise was partially fulfilled when God's Son climbed another mountain outside of Jerusalem called Mount Calvary, and the promise will be completely fulfilled when God establishes His New Jerusalem (see Revelation 3; 21). On Calvary, God provided the final atonement for the sin of mankind.

16. BY MYSELF I HAVE SWORN: "For when God made a promise to Abraham, because He could swear by no one greater, He swore by Himself" (Hebrews 6:13).

17. YOUR DESCENDANTS SHALL POSSESS THE GATE OF THEIR ENEMIES: This metaphor means that the descendants of Abraham would conquer and control their enemies, but it also had an interesting and literal fulfillment in Samson (see Judges 16).

UNLEASHING THE TEXT

1) Put yourself in Abraham's place. How would you have reacted when God commanded you to sacrifice Isaac? What would you have done?

_____

_____

_____

_____

2) Now put yourself in Isaac's place. How would you have felt as you went up the mountain to be sacrificed? Why was Isaac so cooperative with his father?

_____

_____

_____

_____

3) What were God's reasons for commanding Abraham to do this? What were Abraham's reasons for obeying?

_____

_____

_____

_____

4) Why did God send Abraham to Moriah rather than having him perform the sacrifice near where he was living?

_____

_____

_____

_____

EXPLORING THE MEANING

God sometimes calls us to costly obedience. There is no question that Abraham was severely tested by God's command to sacrifice his beloved son. Yet God is not frivolous; this command was not just some random test. His purpose was to prove the strength of Abraham's faith—and a great deal more. He also wanted to present to the world a picture of His plan to sacrifice His own Son on the cross.

God will sometimes ask His children, even in modern times, to obey Him in ways that are costly. The principle He wants us to learn is that faith-filled obedience is more valuable than anything this world has to offer.

The other side to this principle, however, is that costly obedience leads to eternal riches. Abraham's obedience brought a priceless blessing to the entire world, showing mankind just how much God was willing to do to redeem us from death. Our Savior Himself was willing to obey at any cost, and we must be willing to follow His example.

God never gives us tests that we cannot pass. "[God] knows our frame; He remembers that we are dust" (Psalm 103:14). God sends tests to strengthen us and build Christlike character in our lives—not to find fault with us or to seek an excuse to punish us. His tests are designed for us to pass, not to fail.

Of course, when we are in the middle of a trial, it can seem overwhelming and unbearable. At such times we must remember that we have God's Holy Spirit within us, working right alongside us to help us through the trials and tribulations of life. There are times when we are called on merely to endure and trust the Lord—to accept a trial or hardship as from the hand of God without trying to manipulate our way out of it.

"No temptation has overtaken you except such as is common to man; but God is faithful, who will not allow you to be tempted beyond what you are able, but with the temptation will also make the way of escape, that you may be able to bear it" (1 Corinthians 10:13).

God's sacrifice for our sins was costly to both Father and Son. It is interesting that the focus of Genesis 22:1–19 is on Abraham rather than on Isaac. At first glance this may seem strange; after all, it was Isaac who was going to die, not Abraham! But one reason for this is that it gives us a picture of what it cost God the Father to send His only begotten Son to die—slowly and painfully—on the cross at Calvary.

Abraham's long wait for the birth of his beloved son helps us remember how much the Father did to bring His planned Redeemer into our world—only to have Him die a horrible death. Abraham's pain over sacrificing Isaac was nothing compared to what the Father endured when His sinless Son became sin's sacrifice on our behalf.

The cooperation of Isaac and the unity of father and son in this passage are mere glimpses of the perfect unity between the Father, Son, and Holy Spirit. What is most amazing of all is that our God did all this just for the sake of bringing reconciliation with sinners in rebellion against Him. We do serve a great and loving God!

REFLECTING ON THE TEXT

5) In what ways does the sacrifice of Isaac illustrate the sacrifice of Christ? Be specific.

_____

_____

_____

_____

6) Even though Isaac was not sacrificed, what did the ordeal cost Abraham? What did he gain from it? What did others gain?

_____

_____

_____

_____

7) How might things have been different if Abraham had not obeyed God? How did God know that Abraham would obey?

_____

_____

_____

_____

8) How did Abraham know that God would not permanently take Isaac from him? On what did Abraham build his faith?

_____

_____

_____

_____

_____

Personal Response

9) When has God called you to costly obedience? How did you respond? Is there an area of obedience that He is calling you to today?

_____

_____

_____

_____

_____

10) In what ways might God be testing you at present? How can the Holy Spirit provide comfort and strength? Who can you ask for prayer support?

_____

_____

_____

_____

10

JACOB AND ESAU
Genesis 25:19–34; 27:1–40

DRAWING NEAR

As today's reading reveals, sibling rivalries have been around for as long as there have been siblings. What is one rivalry you had in your younger years with a brother, sister, or other close family member? How did that rivalry ultimately work itself out?

_____

_____

_____

_____

THE CONTEXT

We now move forward in time. Abraham and Sarah have died, and Isaac is in the latter years of his life. His wife, Rebekah, is barren, and Isaac pleads with the Lord to open her womb—which He does in duplicate! Rebekah discovers that she has twin boys wrestling inside her, and the Lord prophesies concerning their future.

At the time of these events, Isaac was growing old and infirm. He had already lost his eyesight, and he anticipated that his life was drawing to its close (though it wasn't). He and his family were probably living in Beersheba, where Isaac had spent much of his childhood with Abraham.

An important element in these passages has to do with the birthright of the eldest son. This birthright involved a double portion of the inheritance when the father died, and it also brought a special blessing from father to son. This blessing was at least as important as the material inheritance, and in Isaac's case it was *the most important* element.

The birthright almost invariably was reserved for the firstborn son; only in very special circumstances was it bestowed on another. It was considered a valuable right, something the firstborn son would treasure and insist on as his by birth. It could, however, be bought and sold if a firstborn son were foolish enough to part with it.

This topic is of significance to Christians today because we inherit the birthright of Jesus, God's only begotten Son. This heritage is beyond price; it includes our eternal life in the presence of God the Father.

KEYS TO THE TEXT

Read Genesis 25:19–34, noting the key words and phrases indicated below.

> TWIN NATIONS: *Rebekah is healed of her barrenness and conceives two boys. The Lord then comes to her with a word of prophecy concerning their future.*

25:19. PADAN ARAM: The "plain of Aram" in upper Mesopotamia near Haran.

21. SHE WAS BARREN: Confronted by twenty years of his wife's barrenness, Isaac earnestly turned to God in prayer, obviously acknowledging God's involvement and timing in the seed-promise. God granted his plea.

22. THE CHILDREN STRUGGLED TOGETHER WITHIN HER: Esau would be the firstborn of the twins, with Jacob following immediately after. This struggle that began in the womb would continue between the twin brothers for the rest of their lives.

23. TWO NATIONS ARE IN YOUR WOMB: Esau's descendants were the Ed-omites, who caused problems for the Israelites on and off throughout the Old Testament period. Jacob would become the father of the twelve tribes of Israel after God changed his name from Jacob to Israel.

THE OLDER SHALL SERVE THE YOUNGER: Notice that this prophecy made no mention of the birthright of the elder son; it merely predicted that the elder would serve the younger. The implication is that the Lord's favor would rest with the younger son, but it did not touch on which son *should* receive the birthright.

HAIRY AND HEEL-GRABBER: The sons are born, the first one with lots of hair and the second one grabbing his heel. This heel-grabbing tendency will plague Jacob for most of his life.

25. RED: A ruddy complexion was apparently not common among the Old Testament Jews—although David is also described as "ruddy and good-looking" (1 Samuel 17:42). Some have suggested that Esau's ruddy complexion and hairy body were signs of an excessively passionate nature or a tendency toward cruelty. Esau's adult lifestyle lends some credence to this idea, although the text says nothing to this effect.

ESAU: Probably means "hairy."

26. TOOK HOLD OF ESAU'S HEEL: This gesture would become typical of Jacob's life, as he grew up to be a grasping and conniving person. It is also an interesting foreshadowing of the way he would gain his brother's birthright.

JACOB: Means "heel catcher" or "supplanter."

28. ISAAC LOVED ESAU ... BUT REBEKAH LOVED JACOB: Here we find the beginning of problems, as the parents chose favorites.

MY SOUL FOR SOME STEW: Esau comes home from hunting, feeling tired and hungry—and Jacob is waiting for him. In this shocking passage, Esau demonstrates the foolish shortsightedness of his value system.

29. JACOB COOKED A STEW: We are not told what Jacob's motives were in cooking this stew at this strategic moment. It is possible that he was innocently

making his own supper, yet it is also possible that he planned to tempt his brother, who would be returning shortly from the hunt. In light of Jacob's future acts of cunning, it is quite possible that he had planned in advance to barter for his brother's birthright.

HE WAS WEARY: It is when we are weary—physically or spiritually—that we must be on our guard the most. When our strength is down, so is our ability to recognize and resist temptation.

30. PLEASE FEED ME: This is a legitimate request, insofar as it goes. It is not presumptuous to ask a brother for help in time of need. The problem for Esau, however, is that he would allow his immediate hunger to become a devouring lust.

RED STEW: The Hebrew for this phrase can be transliterated as "red red." This was probably a lentil stew.

HIS NAME WAS CALLED EDOM: This is comparable to "Red," a common enough nickname for redheaded persons even today. Esau's ruddy complexion would have lent itself to this nickname already, but his name will forever become associated with the dreadful decision he was about to make. After this episode the name Edom would remain with him throughout his life, and his descendants would be called the Edomites.

31. SELL ME YOUR BIRTHRIGHT: God had already prophesied that the older would serve the younger (see verse 23), but Jacob was evidently not willing to wait for God to bring this about. By bartering for his brother's birthright, Jacob hoped to switch places with him, making himself equivalent to the firstborn and placing Esau in a subservient position. Jacob would spend much of his adult life learning to trust in God's promises rather than manipulating the circumstances himself.

32. I AM ABOUT TO DIE: Esau was *not* about to die; he was merely hungry and tired. But a habit of immediate gratification caused him to magnify his urges into life-threatening calamities. Esau was evidently accustomed to taking what he needed and satisfying his appetites quickly. This is also a common problem in modern society, where we specialize in instant gratification. Christians are exhorted to deny the flesh in order to prevent our fleshly desires from ruling our lives.

WHAT IS THIS BIRTHRIGHT TO ME: The birthright was a sacred treasure to the firstborn male in Jacob's time. It afforded the firstborn son a double portion of the inheritance when his father died, and it also meant that the father would pronounce a special blessing on his firstborn son and his descendants. We should remember that Isaac did not own any land in Canaan, so Esau's inheritance probably did not seem particularly significant to him at this moment. The bigger and more important portion of his birthright was the spiritual blessing that Isaac would pass on to his son, and this is what Esau was about to spurn.

34. HE ATE AND DRANK, AROSE, AND WENT HIS WAY: Esau will forever epitomize the man who satisfies his physical needs without any concern for his soul.

THUS ESAU DESPISED HIS BIRTHRIGHT: Esau placed more value on the immediate gratification of his physical appetites than he did on the long-range spiritual blessings that were his by right. The full weight of this folly would come home to him soon when he got hungry again. He sold something invaluable for something temporary. It is hard to believe that anyone could make such a foolish bargain—yet we do the same thing when we willfully indulge our fleshly lusts, thereby spurning God's grace and treating His Son's redemption with contempt. We are, in effect, despising our own birthright.

Read Genesis 27:1–40, noting the key words and phrases indicated below.

> FAMILY PLOT: Rebekah now conspires with Jacob to deceive Isaac and steal the birthright from Esau. In this sordid story, the entire family acts badly.

27:2. I DO NOT KNOW THE DAY OF MY DEATH: Isaac actually lived another forty-three years after this event.

4. MAKE ME SAVORY FOOD: Here we discover a pattern, as Isaac himself fell into trouble through a pot of savory stew.

THAT MY SOUL MAY BLESS YOU BEFORE I DIE: Isaac, like his son Esau, was consumed with the urge to satisfy his physical appetites. Esau had claimed that he was about to die when he was merely hungry. Isaac made a similar leap in logic here, as though his death was imminent or his blessing was dependent on having an immediate bowl of venison stew. Some have claimed that Isaac was out of God's will in his desire to bestow the blessings of birthright on Esau, but we must remember that the prophecy concerning the brothers was that the "older shall serve the younger" (Genesis 25:23)—not that the younger would receive the birthright inheritance.

8. OBEY MY VOICE: This phrase shows up repeatedly in the book of Genesis, frequently with negative implications. Adam listened to the voice of his wife and ate the forbidden fruit (see Genesis 3:17). Later he heard the voice of the Lord in the garden of Eden and hid himself (see 3:10). Abram heeded the voice of his wife and produced a son through Hagar—against the Lord's will (see 16:2). Here we find Rebekah giving ungodly advice to her son, and Jacob heeding her words.

10. THAT HE MAY BLESS YOU BEFORE HIS DEATH: Rebekah may have been thinking of the prophecy concerning her sons—that the older would serve the younger—and perhaps she was suddenly filled with fear. Her husband was about to bestow the blessing on the wrong son! It is equally possible, however, that she concocted this scheme simply because Jacob was her favorite. Whatever her motives, her actions were wicked. God's will is not accomplished by mankind's devious schemes.

12. I SHALL SEEM TO BE A DECEIVER TO HIM: The irony of this statement is almost humorous. Jacob was essentially afraid that he would be discovered to be exactly what he was: a base deceiver of his own father. His son Joseph would later demonstrate the correct approach to such temptations by declaring, "How then can I do this great wickedness, and sin against God?" (Genesis 39:9).

13. LET YOUR CURSE BE ON ME: It is possible that Rebekah was acting on a firm conviction that Jacob would be blessed and not cursed, yet her actions were still wrong. We are not to use God's promises to take advantage of others for our own profit. Furthermore, each man is responsible for his own actions. The consequences of Jacob's actions would fall to Jacob, not to his mother—whether she liked it or nor.

19. I AM ESAU YOUR FIRSTBORN: If we have in any way minimized the sin of Jacob and Rebekah previously, there can be no justification any longer. Jacob was lying outright to his own father—blind with the infirmity of old age—claiming to be Esau, saying that the goat stew was actually venison that he had recently taken in the hunt, and disguising his very body with goat hair to mimic his brother's hairy skin.

20. THE LORD YOUR GOD BROUGHT IT TO ME: Jacob's treachery is breathtaking—he had the effrontery to claim that God was involved in this wicked deception of his aged father. Yet here, too, we are forced to recognize that God's people still act in this manner today. "The heart is deceitful above all things, and desperately wicked" (Jeremiah 17:9), and it is easy to justify our own willful actions as being motivated by God's leading. "Let no one say when he is tempted, 'I am tempted by God'; for God cannot be tempted by evil, nor does He Himself tempt anyone. But each one is tempted when he is drawn away by his own desires and enticed" (James 1:13–14).

THE STOLEN BLESSING: Isaac is finally convinced by Jacob's outright lies and bestows the blessing of birthright on him. He also shows that he has forgotten the Lord's prophecy.

27. AND HE CAME NEAR AND KISSED HIM: Finally, with all lingering doubts removed, Isaac pronounced the blessing on Jacob, though the opening words show he thought the one receiving it was Esau, the man of the field. His prayer-wish called for prosperity and superiority and ended with a repeat of God's words to Abraham (see Genesis 12:1–3).

29. BE MASTER OVER YOUR BRETHREN: Isaac himself was not without some culpability in this sordid event, for he certainly understood the Lord's prophecy concerning his sons, which included that Esau and his descendants would serve Jacob, not vice versa. He must also have been aware that Esau had sold the birthright to Jacob, and for better or worse, that was a binding contract—Isaac was as bound to recognize it as Esau was. Furthermore, Esau had married Canaanite women (see Genesis 26:34–35), which had brought much grief to his parents. In many ways, Isaac should have realized that Jacob had been chosen of God, and this blessing ought to have gone to him.

CURSED BE EVERYONE WHO CURSES YOU, AND BLESSED BE THOSE WHO BLESS YOU: This may be a stock bit of phrasing in the blessings that fathers bestowed on their sons, yet it is almost verbatim of the blessing that the Lord bestowed on Abraham. It suggests that Isaac was expecting the chosen seed to continue through Esau—perhaps through both Esau and Jacob. But Esau had already removed himself from that plan by selling his birthright.

33. ISAAC TREMBLED EXCEEDINGLY: Isaac was visibly shocked when Esau entered the tent and uncovered the scandal. Remembering the Lord's words to Rebekah (see 25:23), he refused to withdraw the blessing and emphatically affirmed its validity, telling Esau that indeed Jacob would be blessed and that he would serve his brother.

WEEPING WON'T BRING IT BACK: Esau finally comes face-to-face with the monumental folly he committed by selling his birthright. In many ways he is a picture of those who reject Christ.

34. BLESS ME—ME ALSO: Esau fully expected to receive the blessing, for he had identified himself to his father as the firstborn. In his anguish at losing this important paternal blessing, and bitterly acting as the innocent victim, Esau shifted the blame for the loss to Jacob and pleaded for some compensating word of blessing from his father.

35. TAKEN AWAY YOUR BLESSING: Esau did receive a blessing from his father, but it was not the blessing of birthright. There can be only one such blessing, and once bestowed, it can never be removed. This aspect of the birthright blessing is a wonderful picture of the security of our birthright as Christians. Our rebirth into the family of Christ brings us all the blessings of His birthright as the only begotten Son of God—and this inheritance and blessing can never be taken away from us.

38. ESAU LIFTED UP HIS VOICE AND WEPT: Realizing the irrevocable nature of what had happened, Esau responded with both anger and grief. Like Esau, those who reject the spiritual birthright that God offers through His Son, Jesus Christ, will also one day weep over the irreversible consequences of their rejection. When we accept Christ's atonement for our sins, we are brought into the family of God and inherit the full blessing and birthright of the Son of God. But there will come a day when those who have rejected this gift will be cast "into the furnace of fire. There will be wailing and gnashing of teeth" (Matthew 13:42).

40. YOU SHALL BREAK HIS YOKE FROM YOUR NECK: In later history, the Edomites, who descended from the line of Esau, fought time and again with Israel and shook off Israelite control on several occasions (see 2 King 8:20; 2 Chronicles 21:8–10; 28:16–17).

Unleashing the Text

1) Why might Esau have been so willing to sell his birthright? Why did he not consider it valuable?

_____

_____

_____

_____

2) Why did Jacob play such a trick on his brother just for the sake of the birthright?

_____

_____

_____

_____

_____

3) Whose sin is worse in your opinion: Jacob's or Esau's? Why?

_____

_____

_____

_____

_____

4) If you had been in Isaac's position, how would you have responded to Jacob and Rebekah's conspiracy?

_____

_____

_____

_____

EXPLORING THE MEANING

The birthright of Jesus is eternal life. Every human on earth is born from the seed of Adam, which means that every one of us is under the curse of sin and death. But God sent His Son to bring us a new birth, allowing us to be born again into the family of God. When we are, we immediately receive the full blessing and birthright that the Father has in store for His Son—and this includes eternal life and freedom from the curse of death.

But this birthright is only passed on to those who are of the family of God, who have been born again into faith in Jesus Christ. It is, therefore, entirely possible to miss the opportunity, to treat this birthright with contempt as though it were not even as valuable as temporal pleasure or immediate gratification. This may not be the conscious train of logic that people have in mind when they refuse to accept Christ, but it is, in fact, what they are doing.

We must never treat God's grace with contempt lest we become like Esau, who treated his own birthright with such derision. In the end, he realized his dreadful mistake—but he realized it too late. He could not buy it back, even with weeping and anguish. If you accomplish nothing else in life, make sure you don't miss out on the birthright of eternal life through Jesus Christ. We must not be like "Esau, who for one morsel of food sold his birthright. For you know that afterward, when he wanted to inherit the blessing, he was rejected, for he found no place for repentance, though he sought it diligently with tears" (Hebrews 12:16–17).

God's purposes are not furthered by our manipulative schemes. God had intended from the beginning that Esau be subservient to Jacob. He promised it before the boys were born and would have accomplished it *without* any plots from Isaac's family. We saw the same principle in the life of Abraham: he had God's promise of an heir through his wife Sarah, yet he allowed his fears (and his wife's schemes) to override his faith in God's word.

In each of these cases, the schemes of men led to bad consequences. Jacob's schemes alienated him from his twin brother for the rest of his life and led to his being deceived repeatedly by others. Abraham's involvement with Hagar led to a deep-seated enmity between Arabs and Israelis that is very much alive even today.

God accomplishes what He promises. This does not mean that we are not involved in those promises, but our involvement requires *obedience,* not scheming. Our involvement may sometimes require no effort at all on our part—except for placing our faith in God's provision. Indeed, as we have seen in this study, this effort often proves the most difficult.

The pleasures and cares of this world are temporary, but God's blessings are eternal. Esau possessed something that had tremendous long-term value in the blessing of his father—a blessing that carries down even into modern times. Yet he sold this priceless blessing for something that lasted less than a day. Within a few hours, Esau was probably hungry again.

The world offers countless pleasures, opportunities, and distractions, and life brings many forms of sorrow, suffering, and worry—but none of these things will last. We must be always on our guard so that we do not behave like Esau, letting go of the priceless relationship we have with the Father in exchange for some fleeting sensual pleasure. Further, we should never allow the sorrows and cares of this world to persuade us that God is not involved, that He does not care about His children, or that He has forgotten His promises.

The Christian's birthright is to enjoy the intimacy with the Father that Jesus Himself enjoys—perfect and complete and eternally secure. We must remember the example of Esau and take care to not exchange that for anything in the world.

REFLECTING ON THE TEXT

5) Consider each member of Isaac's family. What led each to doubt or forget
   God's word? What led each to treat His promises with contempt?

Isaac:

_____

_____

_____

_____

Jacob:

_____

_____

_____

_____

Esau:

_____

_____

_____

Rebekah:

_____

_____

_____

_____

_____

6) What were each person's top priorities?

_____

_____

_____

_____

_____

7) How do you resolve Jacob's lies and deceit with the fact that he was chosen
   by God to bring about the line of Christ?

_____

_____

_____

_____

_____

8) What did each person in the family lose in the passages we've studied? What did each gain?

Isaac:

_____

_____

_____

_____

_____

Jacob:

_____

_____

_____

_____

Esau:

_____

_____

_____

_____

Rebekah:

_____

_____

_____

_____

PERSONAL RESPONSE

9) Have you accepted the birthright of eternal life through Jesus? If not, what is holding you back?

_____

_____

_____

_____

10) What is your top priority in life at present? What things are hindering or endangering your relationship with God?

_____

_____

_____

_____

11

WRESTLING WITH GOD
Genesis 28:10–22; 32:1–33:17

DRAWING NEAR

Jacob was a man who liked to make deals—even deals with God. In what ways have you been guilty in the past of trying to "bargain" with God?

_____

_____

_____

_____

THE CONTEXT

In the previous study, we saw how Jacob stole his brother's birthright by guile. Esau was angry, understandably, and vowed to kill Jacob. So Jacob's parents sent him off to live with his mother's brother Laban for a time. Our passage opens with Jacob heading off to his uncle's—but he had an unexpected meeting with God along the way.

Jacob eventually arrived at his uncle Laban's home and spent many years working there, tending sheep and livestock for his uncle. During this time he became very wealthy by using some rather devious tricks to enrich himself

137

from his father-in-law's flocks. But he also found himself on the receiving end of crafty guile when he fell in love with Rachel, Laban's younger daughter. He agreed to work for seven years to attain her hand in marriage, but when the wedding day arrived, Uncle Laban treacherously substituted older sister Leah instead of Jacob's beloved Rachel. Jacob was forced to work for another seven years to gain the hand of Rachel as his second wife.

Tensions and distrust also began to breed within Jacob's family. He demonstrated love toward Rachel while making poor Leah feel unloved and unwanted. So God consoled her with many children, while Rachel remained barren. Needless to say, this created further tension and resentment within the home. Jacob bore the brunt of the bitterness and heartache of his two wives—and several concubines for good measure.

After many years, when Jacob was nearly one hundred years old, he found himself forced to leave his uncle's household. Family friction and suspicion had increased to the point where the two men could no longer live together. So Jacob headed back toward Bethel, where he had met God many years before. Unfortunately, his brother Esau learned of his arrival and rode out to meet him—with four hundred men in his company! Jacob found himself caught between two men whom he had swindled, and in desperation he finally called on the name of the Lord.

Jacob's treachery and deceit were coming back to torment him, but God had a great blessing in store as well.

KEYS TO THE TEXT

Read Genesis 28:10–22, noting the key words and phrases indicated below.

JACOB'S DREAM: Esau had vowed to kill Jacob for his treachery, so his parents send him off to live with his uncle Laban. Along the way, he stops for the night.

28:11. A CERTAIN PLACE: Haran (see map in the Introduction).

12. A LADDER: This dream offers a graphic portrayal of the Lord's personal involvement in the affairs of the earth, and here especially as they related to divine covenant promises in Jacob's life (see Genesis 28:13–15). This dream

was to encourage the lonely traveler. God's own appointed angelic messengers carried out His will and plans. More than likely, the angels traversed a stairway rather than a ladder.

13. I WILL GIVE TO YOU: God now repeated for Jacob the same promises He had given to Abraham. Jacob would inherit the land, his descendants would be innumerable, and his descendants would become a blessing to the nations.

14. YOUR DESCENDANTS SHALL BE AS THE DUST OF THE EARTH: The Lord here revealed a new detail that we have not encountered before: Jacob's descendants would "spread abroad to the west and the east, to the north and the south," effectively filling the earth. This prophecy came to pass during the period known as the *Dispersion* when the Jews were scattered throughout the earth. It will be fulfilled more fully during the Millennial Kingdom when Christ reigns for a thousand years over the earth from Jerusalem.

15. BRING YOU BACK TO THIS LAND: God told Abraham that his descendants would be enslaved in a foreign land for four hundred years, after which time they would return to the Promised Land (see Genesis 15:13–16). This prophecy was fulfilled after the Israelites' exodus out of Egypt.

JACOB'S PICTURE OF GOD: Jacob awakens after his dream and responds to the Lord's visit. But his response indicates that he does not understand the God of his fathers very well.

16. THE LORD IS IN THIS PLACE: It seems that Jacob did not understand that God is everywhere at all times—He is omnipresent. He may have pictured God as moving about like a man, as that is the physical form He took on at least one occasion with Abraham. Jacob seemed to be saying here that God lived in Bethel and that if one moved away from Bethel, he would be moving away from God. There is no doubt that Jacob had much to learn concerning the God of his fathers.

18. SET IT UP AS A PILLAR: It was a known practice in Jacob's day to mark a particular site as of special religious significance by means of a stone pillar. A libation offering (anointing the stone with oil), a change of place-name, and a vow of allegiance to the Lord in exchange for promised protection and blessing completed Jacob's ceremonial consecration of Bethel.

19. BETHEL: Meaning "house of God."

MAKING DEALS WITH GOD: Though Jacob sets up a pillar to commemorate God's visitation and even renames the place, he is overcome with his own distrust and tries to bargain with God.

20. IF GOD WILL BE WITH ME: God had just promised in the clearest terms that He would be with Jacob—yet Jacob was struggling to have faith in that promise. Abraham had a similar encounter with God; however, Abraham "believed in the LORD, and He accounted it to him for righteousness" (Genesis 15:6). It would appear that Isaac had not passed on to his son the truths of God's character that he himself experienced. Jacob's bad character also hindered him. He had been deceitful and treacherous to others, including his own twin brother, and expected others to treat him in the same way. Men who are not trustworthy have a difficult time trusting others—including God, the only One who is absolutely trustworthy.

21. THEN THE LORD SHALL BE MY GOD: This is a response to God's miraculous appearance that we have not seen before. The Lord had just given Jacob a dramatic vision of Himself and had reiterated a promise He had given to Jacob's father and grandfather. If Jacob knew the facts of God's interactions with Abraham and Isaac and of the dramatic miracles that God had worked in the lives of his forebears—such as Isaac's miraculous birth and subsequent sacrifice—then we would expect him to bow in worship as Abraham had done. Instead, Jacob was trying to make a deal with God, effectively saying, "If You will keep Your promise, *then* I will make You my God—but not otherwise."

Read Genesis 32:1–33:17, noting the key words and phrases indicated below.

THE PAST CATCHES UP: Years pass, and Jacob and Laban eventually decide to part ways. Jacob journeys with his wives and children back to Bethel, but along the way he unexpectedly meets his angry brother, Esau.

32:1. THE ANGELS OF GOD: With the suspense of having to face Esau before him, Jacob was met by an angelic host. They must have reminded him of Bethel, which served also as a timely reminder and encouragement of God's will being done on earth.

2. GOD'S CAMP ... MAHANAIM: Meaning "double camp," that is, one being God's and one being his own.

3. SEIR ... EDOM: The territory of Esau south of the Dead Sea.

7. JACOB WAS GREATLY AFRAID: Much time had passed in Jacob's life since his dream of God's ladder from heaven. He had cheated his father-in-law and been severely cheated in return, and over the years he had begun to learn some lessons in godliness. Now Jacob learned that his brother, Esau, was coming to meet him with four hundred men. He was stricken with fear that Esau intended to kill him for his birthright treachery.

9. O GOD OF MY FATHER ABRAHAM: Up until now, Jacob had generally taken matters into his own hands, using whatever means he chose to accomplish his goals. But here we see a change of heart beginning: he was learning to call on the name of God when he was in distress. It is also significant that he now addressed God as "God of my father Abraham and God of my father Isaac." It suggests that he had gained a deeper knowledge of the One whom he served, and it was also his first recorded prayer since his dream in Bethel.

10. I AM NOT WORTHY: Jacob was learning humility. His lifelong habit of cunning and conniving had grown out of pride—a pride that led him to believe that he could take charge of his own life without God's help. His previous encounter with God also demonstrated that pride, as he responded to God's grace by trying to make a deal. The wheeler-dealer is not apparent any longer.

11. DELIVER ME, I PRAY: Here we have a great breakthrough in Jacob's life. In the past he would have met such a crisis with cunning and craftiness, but now he called on his God to intervene on his behalf.

THE HAND OF ESAU: Jacob had good reason to be afraid, for he remembered the wicked way he treated his twin brother many years ago—and his brother's vow to kill him (see Genesis 27).

THE MOTHER WITH THE CHILDREN: Jacob expected that Esau would slaughter his entire household—men, women, and children. Men who spend their lives in deceit and treachery will generally expect others to behave the same way, which causes them to be distrustful and suspicious of everyone. Jacob would never overcome this side effect to his own craftiness.

12. **For You said:** God likes to be reminded of His own words, and Jacob here reminds Him of His promise at Bethel. Again, this is the first time Jacob reminded God of these things or showed any real interest in submitting himself to God's plan.

13-20. **He ... took what came to his hand:** The logistics of Jacob's careful appeasement strategy (550 animals that Esau would prize) may highlight his ability to plan, but it highlights even more his failure to pray and believe that God would change Esau's heart.

Jacob Hides: Jacob divides his household and flocks into two groups and sends them out ahead of him. Then he sends out his wives and children. He himself cowers behind.

21. **The present went on over before him:** Jacob had put together a huge gift for Esau in hopes that the bribe would turn away his wrath. Jacob, of course, did not know that Esau was coming in friendship and forgiveness rather than vengeance. He could not expect Esau's reaction, for Jacob would never have done such a thing himself. Indeed, he had sent on his family—his wives and children—to bear the brunt of Esau's wrath, while he shrank to the background.

22. **Jabbok:** A stream, sixty to sixty-five miles long, east of the Jordan River. It flows into that river midway between the Sea of Galilee and the Dead Sea.

24. **Jacob was left alone:** This is the natural result of a life of treachery and selfishness; such a man will one day realize that he is completely alone. Fortunately for Jacob, however, he was not truly alone—the Lord was with him, just as He promised. And there was also a certain pathos in this picture, as Jacob prayed in lonely exile the night before his ordeal.

Wrestling with God: Suddenly we are confronted with a strange meeting, as God comes to Jacob—and Jacob wrestles Him to the ground. This provides an interesting contrast to Abraham.

A Man wrestled with him: This Man was none other than God Himself. This appearance to Jacob was in stark contrast with God's appearance to Abraham in Mamre when Abraham interceded for the people of Sodom (see Genesis 18). Jacob did not stand before the Lord nor draw near to His face; he grappled and wrestled on the ground. He did not intercede for others; on the contrary, he sent others—women and children—out in front to intercede for him! Jacob was growing in godliness, but he was still a very self-centered man.

UNTIL THE BREAKING OF DAY: Again, this is a dramatic antithesis to Abraham's encounter with God. Abraham "wrestled" in a figurative sense with God, trying to understand the mind of his Creator. Jacob, however, spent the entire night trying to force *his* will onto God. This is how he lived his life, forcing his will on others, and it had severely damaged his relationship with God and all those close to him.

> JACOB BECOMES ISRAEL: *Jacob reveals the depth of his heart as he begs for God's blessing. God grants that boon and gives him a new name in the process.*

26. UNLESS YOU BLESS ME: God had already blessed Jacob—the sad irony is that He appeared to Jacob this time to bless him still *further*. Nevertheless, we see in this request where Jacob's heart lay: he longed for God's blessing and yearned to be a friend of God, as his grandfather Abraham had been. This is also what God saw in Jacob. He looked beneath the conniving surface to the godly yearning in his heart.

28. YOU ... HAVE PREVAILED: There is a positive example to be found in Jacob's wrestling, although it grew out of a character weakness in his case. Christians are exhorted to be fervent and persistent in prayer (see Luke 18; James 5:16), imitating Jacob's example of perseverance and tenacity.

30. PENIEL: Meaning "face of God."

> RESTORATION: *The following day after Jacob's wrestling match with God, he limps across the river to face Esau.*

33:1. ESAU WAS COMING: Jacob hastily divided his family into three groups and went ahead of them to meet his brother.

2. RACHEL AND JOSEPH LAST: The division and relative location of Jacob's family in relationship to the perceived danger gives tremendous insight into whom he favored.

3. BOWED HIMSELF TO THE GROUND ... ESAU RAN TO MEET HIM: Jacob approached his brother fearfully and deferentially, as an inferior would

a highly honored patron, while Esau ran to greet his brother without restraint of emotion.

5–9. WHO ARE THESE WITH YOU: Jacob properly acknowledged God's gracious provision as he introduced his large family and explained his gift to Esau of the 550 animals.

10. THE FACE OF GOD: Jacob noticed how God had so obviously changed Esau, as indicated by his facial expression, which was not one of sullen hate but of brotherly love.

15. LET ME FIND FAVOR: Jacob did not want to have Esau's people loaned to him for fear something might happen to again fracture their relationship.

16–17. TO SEIR ... TO SUCCOTH: Jacob courteously dismissed Esau's escort, and they parted company. For whatever reason, Jacob's expressed intention to meet his brother again in Seir did not materialize. Instead, he halted his journey first at Succoth, and then at Shechem.

UNLEASHING THE TEXT

1) What sort of neighbor might Jacob have been if he lived near you? What would he be like as a coworker or employee?

_____

_____

_____

_____

2) What does Jacob's dream mean? What is the ladder? Who or what are the angels going up and down the ladder?

_____

_____

_____

_____

3) Why did Jacob try to bargain with God after his dream? What does this show about his character? What does it show about his understanding of God?

_____

_____

_____

_____

4) What would you have done if you had been in Jacob's place, anticipating that Esau was on his way to kill you?

_____

_____

_____

EXPLORING THE MEANING

When we insist on taking matters into our own hands, we cheat ourselves of God's full blessing. Jacob was a man of God, and he was the man who became known as Israel. He was blessed of God, yet he robbed himself of many more blessings that could have been his.

Jacob lived a life marked by deceit and trickery, and that caused him to expect others to be deceitful and treacherous with him. As a result, he found it difficult to trust God. He doubted God's promises, and he attempted to secure a blessing by force that God wanted to give him freely. He stands in marked contrast to his grandfather Abraham, who took God at His word and found Him faithful.

We tend to expect others to treat us the way we treat them. If we tend to manipulate others into doing what we want, we will wind up unable to trust people—and God. God will still be faithful, but we will cheat ourselves of the blessings of intimacy and trust.

God still uses us despite our failures and weaknesses. This is the "good news" part of the previous principle, and we see it illustrated in Jacob's life. Jacob was a man with many obvious weaknesses and shortcomings, and from a human perspective he was not the sort of man that most people would trust. But God was still able to use him in mighty ways, and he is listed among the heroes of the faith.

"The LORD does not see as man sees; for man looks at the outward appearance, but the LORD looks at the heart" (1 Samuel 16:7). The Lord looked on the heart of Jacob and found a man who ultimately longed for His blessing and intimacy.

When we have a relationship with our Creator, He instills within us character traits that are pleasing to Him. Through His Spirit He develops those things in us, making us more like Christ as we grow. This process may not always be pleasant, but in the end we will reflect the image of His Son.

Parents must teach their children about God's character. Jacob's early responses to God seem to suggest that he had little knowledge of God's character. His verbal response seemed to be closer to a business deal than to worship and praise.

This again was radically different from the responses of his grandfather Abraham, who had a clear understanding of the persona and character of the Lord. Somewhere along the line, it would appear that Jacob had not been taught very clearly about God. Perhaps Isaac forgot to teach him about all the things that he had seen God do in his own life and in Abraham's life. As a result, it took Jacob a lifetime to discover the fullness of God's grace and mercy, and he wasted a lot of time wrestling against both God and man.

Each person must come to repentance and salvation for himself—the fact that a parent is a Christian does not guarantee the salvation of his children. Yet parents who teach their children about God's love and salvation lay a critical spiritual foundation for them. In faithfully teaching their kids about the gospel, they pass on a genuine blessing and "birthright" to their children.

REFLECTING ON THE TEXT

5) Why did Jacob wrestle with God? Why did God consent to wrestle with Jacob?

_____

_____

_____

_____

6) What might have happened if Jacob had **not** wrestled with God? What sort of meeting might they have had? Why did Jacob's stubborn, manipulative character make a wrestling match necessary?

_____

_____

_____

_____

7) Why do you think God gave Jacob a limp during the wrestling match? In what ways did Jacob's limp serve as a constant reminder of his weakness and of his need to depend on God?

_____

_____

_____

_____

8) Given Jacob's untrustworthy character, why did God bless him? In what ways did Jacob experience the fruit of his sinfulness?

_____

_____

_____

_____

PERSONAL RESPONSE

9) Is there an area in your life where you are wrestling against God? How can you let go and trust Him more fully?

_____

_____

_____

_____

10) Are there ways that "wrestling" with God is a good thing? What does this teach us about prayer?

_____

_____

_____

_____

12

REVIEWING KEY PRINCIPLES

DRAWING NEAR

As you look back at each of the studies in Genesis 12–33, what is the one thing that stood out to you the most? What is one new perspective you have learned?

_____

_____

_____

_____

THE CONTEXT

We have examined the lives of the great patriarchs of the faith—Abraham, Isaac, and Jacob (Israel)—and have seen how each of them learned to walk by faith rather than by sight. Each of these people had strengths and weaknesses, and each was made of the same flesh that we are made of. They were all people just like us, struggling with the realities of life in a fallen world and learning to trust in their faithful Creator.

The major theme of these studies has been on what is required to live by faith and what is gained by such a lifestyle. The central tenet of this lifestyle is to trust in the character of God, not in the evidences of our senses or the circumstances of the world around us. God is always faithful, and He will always keep His promises. Those promises include an eternal life in His kingdom, blessed with His presence for all eternity. This is available through His Son, Jesus Christ, who through the cross provides the only way to peace with God.

The following represents a few of the major themes we have found. There are many more that we don't have room to reiterate, so take some time to review the earlier studies—or, better still, to meditate on the passages in Scripture that we have covered. Ask the Holy Spirit to give you wisdom and insight into His Word.

EXPLORING THE MEANING

God calls His people to walk in faith. Each of the characters we have looked at in these studies was called on to believe the promises of God—promises that appeared to be utterly impossible. God then asked them to take some action based on those promises, and this action is what we call "walking in faith."

To walk in faith means to step into the unknown, even into threatening circumstances, with only God's Word to depend on. Abraham arrived in Canaan to find himself surrounded with unfriendly people, and then God told him that he would inherit the entire land for his descendants. Later he was called on to sacrifice his son, even though all God's promises for the future depended on that son.

Walking in faith requires that we accept God's Word at face value, even when it seems impossible that His promises can come true. In this, the patriarchs provide us with great role models.

God works all things together for good to those who trust Him. This principle is closely related to the previous one in that we are called to trust and obey. But the good news is that God's long-term plans for the human race do not override His short-term plans for us as individuals.

God's promises to Abraham focused more on his descendants than they did on him personally. The land of Canaan was promised to his offspring, but he personally never received any place that he could call home. But at the same time, Abraham was given something far greater than any piece of real estate: he was granted a saving relationship with God Himself.

The Lord does use His people to further His purposes in the lives of others, but He also pours out blessings on those people as He uses them. The greatest blessing of all is free to God's people today, just as it was for Abraham: an intimate communion with the Creator of all things.

The comforts of the world can become a deadly trap. Lot did not leave Abraham and head straight for a new house in Sodom; rather, he arrived there by degrees. So it is with the comforts and entanglements of the world—they grow on us a little at a time.

This is a difficult balance, because the Lord's people are called to be in the world but not of the world (see John 17:14–16). We have no choice but to live in society and take part in the workaday economy, yet we must also be on guard to ensure that these entanglements do not become the focus of our lives.

"Do not love the world or the things in the world. If anyone loves the world, the love of the Father is not in him. For all that is in the world—the lust of the flesh, the lust of the eyes, and the pride of life—is not of the Father but is of the world. And the world is passing away, and the lust of it; but he who does the will of God abides forever" (1 John 2:15–17).

God sometimes calls us to costly obedience. There is no question that Abraham was severely tested by God's command to sacrifice his beloved son. Yet God is not frivolous, and this command was not just some random test. God's purpose was to prove the strength of Abraham's faith—and a great deal more. He also wanted to present to the world a picture of His plan to sacrifice His own Son on the cross.

God will sometimes ask His children, even in modern times, to obey Him in ways that are very costly. Sometimes obedience to His Word requires great personal sacrifice. But we can be confident that obedience is more valuable than anything this world has to offer. Moreover, as the record of the faithful in Hebrews 11 reveals, costly obedience leads to eternal riches.

God never gives us tests we cannot pass. "[God] knows our frame; He remembers that we are dust" (Psalm 103:14). God sends tests into our lives to strengthen us and build Christlike character in our lives—not to find fault with us or to seek an excuse to punish us. His tests are designed for us to pass, not to fail.

Of course, when we are in the middle of a trial, it can seem overwhelming and unbearable. At such times, we must remember that Christians have God's Holy Spirit within us, working right alongside of us to help us through the trials and tribulations of life. There are times when we are called on to patiently endure, to accept a trial or hardship as from the hand of God without trying to manipulate the circumstances in order to contrive our own solutions.

"My brethren, count it all joy when you fall into various trials, knowing that the testing of your faith produces patience" (James 1:2–3). "No temptation has overtaken you except such as is common to man; but God is faithful, who will not allow you to be tempted beyond what you are able, but with the temptation will also make the way of escape, that you may be able to bear it" (1 Corinthians 10:13).

We are all called to be friends of God. It is easy to become complacent about this concept and take for granted what a priceless treasure we have in our relationship with God through Christ. When we pray, we are entering freely into the presence of the Creator of the universe! This is a privilege that came at tremendous cost—the painful death of God's own Son—and we Christians can easily forget how privileged we are.

As God's friends, we are invited to reverentially and respectfully enter His presence at any time. More than this, we are urged to do so, as God is actually eager to fellowship with us!

Abraham demonstrated the proper attitude toward this incredible blessing when he stood with God to speak as a man speaks to a friend—and then stepped even closer to speak to Him intimately. This attitude is both pleasing to God and profitable to His children.

God knows our doubts, but He rewards our faith. Both Abraham and Sarah had doubts and misgivings about God's promise concerning an heir. Both of them responded in mocking laughter, and both of them attempted at one time to take matters into their own hands. But in the end they believed God, and God confirmed their faith when Isaac was born.

Jacob had an imperfect understanding of the character of God, and his life was filled with cunning and trickery. Yet in the end he learned to rely on God's character, believing by faith that He would keep His promises—even when Jacob's common sense urged him to take matters into his own hands. God is looking for men and women of faith—men and women who are looking toward His Son, Jesus Christ. As we take small steps of faith, He is faithful to grow us more into the image of our Savior.

This world is not our home. It is vital that Christians keep this truth in mind, for we are called to keep our eyes focused on eternity rather than on the world. But the world has a way of insinuating itself and its values into our thinking. Careers, academics, bills, obligations, even family will all demand our time and attention. This is a fact of life and cannot be entirely avoided while we live in the world. But we must also remember that we are *in* the world but not *of* the world—our home is in eternity.

This mindset is one that must be renewed frequently, because the world around us will not give up the battle for our minds. We renew our minds by immersing ourselves in Scripture and by surrounding ourselves with other Christians who are like-minded. We reinforce the frame of mind by remembering, whenever we are tempted to worry or covet, that we are not going to be living on this planet forever.

We are citizens of a heavenly city, one that is not built by human hands and one that will last forever. Everything in this world—absolutely everything—will one day be destroyed by fire, and we must take care not to invest our lives into things that will be burned up.

Unleashing the Text

1) Which of the concepts or principles in this study have you found to be the most encouraging? Why?

_____

_____

_____

_____

_____

2) Which of the concepts or principles have you found most challenging? Why?

_____

_____

_____

_____

3) What aspects of "walking with God" are you already doing in your life? Which areas need strengthening?

_____

_____

_____

_____

4) To which of the characters that we've studied have you most been able to relate? How might you emulate that person in your own life?

_____

_____

_____

_____

_____

PERSONAL RESPONSE

5) Have you taken a definite stand for Jesus Christ? Have you accepted His free gift of salvation? If not, what is preventing you?

_____

_____

_____

_____

6) In which areas of your life have you been the most convicted during this study? What exact things will you do to address these convictions? Be specific.

_____

_____

_____

_____

7) What have you learned about the character of God during this study? How has this insight affected your worship or prayer life?

_____

_____

_____

_____

_____

8) What are some specific things that you want to see God do in your life during the coming month? What are some things that you intend to change in your own life during that time? (Return to this list in one month and hold yourself accountable to fulfill these things.)

_____

_____

_____

_____

If you would like to continue in your study of Genesis, read the next title in this series: _Genesis 34–50: Jacob and Egypt._

ALSO AVAILABLE

JOHN MACARTHUR

GENESIS
1–11

CREATION, SIN AND THE NATURE OF GOD

MacArthur Bible Studies

I n this study, John MacArthur guides readers through an
in-depth look at the creation story, the first murder, Noah
and the Flood, the first covenant, the Tower of Babel, and
the dispersion of the nations. This study includes close-up
examinations of Adam, Eve, Cain, Abel, and Noah, as well as
careful considerations of doctrinal themes such as "The Fall
of Man" and "Heritage and Family."

The MacArthur Bible Studies provide intriguing examinations of the whole of Scripture. Each guide incorporates
extensive commentary, detailed observations on overriding
themes, and probing questions to help you study the Word of
God with guidance from John MacArthur.

Also Available

JOHN MACARTHUR

GENESIS
34–50

JACOB AND EGYPT

MacArthur Bible Studies

In this study, John MacArthur guides readers through an in-depth look at the historical period beginning with Jacob's first encounter with Rachel, continuing through their son Joseph's captivity as an Egyptian slave, and concluding with the dramatic rescue of Jacob's family. This study includes close-up examinations of Dinah (Jacob's daughter), Judah, Tamar, and Pharaoh's chief butler, as well as careful considerations of doctrinal themes such as "The Sovereignty of God" and "Finishing in Faith."

The MacArthur Bible Studies provide intriguing examinations of the whole of Scripture. Each guide incorporates extensive commentary, detailed observations on overriding themes, and probing questions to help you study the Word of God with guidance from John MacArthur.

ALSO AVAILABLE

I n this study, John MacArthur guides readers through an in-depth look at the historical period beginning with God's calling of Moses, continuing through the giving of the Ten Commandments, and concluding with the Israelites' preparations to enter the Promised Land. This study includes close-up examinations of Aaron, Caleb, Joshua, Balaam and Balak, as well as careful considerations of doctrinal themes such as "Complaints and Rebellion" and "Following God's Law."

The MacArthur Bible Studies provide intriguing examinations of the whole of Scripture. Each guide incorporates extensive commentary, detailed observations on overriding themes, and probing questions to help you study the Word of God with guidance from John MacArthur.